THE LEADER'S CODE

The Leader's Code

Ken Chapman, Ph.D.

iUniverse, Inc.

New York Lincoln Shanghai

The Leader's Code

iUniverse, Inc.

For information address:
iUniverse, Inc.
2021 Pine Lake Road, Suite 100
Lincoln, NE 68512
www.iuniverse.com

ISBN: 0-595-29587-8 (pbk)
ISBN: 0-595-66025-8 (cloth)

Printed in the United States of America

For Jeremiah George Chapman

Contents

Author's Preface

The Leader's Code is about the principles which have guided the best leaders across the years. The best leaders have always led by example by first leading themselves. Having mastered the art of self-management, the best leaders turn their attention to those who would choose to follow them. But the first concern of the best leaders is to lead one's self and to lead one's self well.

The final days of the American Revolutionary War give us a compelling example. The officers of the Continental Army had not been paid for several months. Unlike many members of the Continental Congress, the officers were not men of wealth. They were small farmers and merchants who had creditors to satisfy and mortgages to meet. They were in urgent need of having their salaries paid. The Continental Congress, on the other hand, was flat broke. The Congress pleaded with the officers: "Give us thirty days. The British know they are beaten. They will sign the peace treaty any day now and the French Government will issue our young republic letters of credit and we will pay you in full. However, you must stay with your troops so that the British Army will know we are willing to continue the fight if necessary."

Having heard the plea of the Continental Congress, the officers refused to wait. The officers began making plans to march on the Congress meeting in session in New York. Anxious to avoid a confrontation, the Congress sent an urgent dispatch to General Washington. The Congress asked Washington to intercede. The messenger rode through the night and arrived at Washington's headquarters shortly before seven a.m. After reading the congressional request, Washington asked where the officers were meeting. Learning that they were assembled in a nearby barn, he rode immediately to speak with them. When he arrived, he requested the opportunity to address the officers. The request was quickly granted. Standing before the assembled officers, General Washington took the congressional dispatch from his breast pocket and began to read. He had read only a few words when a senior staff officer interrupted, "General, you don't have to read the rest of the letter. We will wait." General Washington's biographer tells us the officers waited because they all knew that throughout the course of the war, Washington had never been paid. Whenever money was available from the Continental Congress, Washington had always insisted that his soldiers and then his officers be paid. Even more, at the darkest moment of the war, Washington had mortgaged his beloved Mount Vernon in order to pay the salaries of his men. The Continental Congress would eventually settle accounts with Washington. He would be paid for his service, and he would recover the mortgage on Mount Vernon. However, that day in that barn, Washington had never been paid and the assembled officers knew it. "The officers waited," states Washington's biographer, "because not a single man could think of a verbal argument to match the witness of General Washington's behavior."

The leader's code which guided General Washington is expounded in the pages which follow. Leaders first lead themselves. Leaders then focus on leading others to lead themselves. The personal influence which makes these two principles effective is found in the time-tested principle of *leading by example*. Leading by example is what *The Leader's Code* is all about.

THE LEADER'S CODE

A leader has faith in the magic of the human heart.
A leader believes in what people are like at their best.

A leader is patient with people as they learn and grow.
Leaders treat others as they would like to be treated.

A leader is supportive.
A leader voluntarily seeks to be helpful to others.

A leader is trustworthy.
Leaders manage their own words and behavior.
A leader self-corrects.

A leader is loyal to the best interest of the common good.
A leader is guided by an abiding faith in right.

A leader empathizes with others.
A leader seeks to understand others.

A leader speaks less and listens more.
A leader listens to understand.
A leader speaks to clarify and build trust.

A leader is honest, rational and civil.
A leader values common sense.
A leader honors basic human dignity.

A leader leads others to lead themselves.

A leader is candid.
A leader tells the truth with compassion.

A leader is a peacemaker and a coalition builder.

A leader is a team player who can follow as well as lead.
A leader understands the task of team building.

1

Leaders Know People Matter

A leader has faith in the magic of the human heart.
A leader believes in what people are like at their best.

People have an intrinsic need to be valued. Businesses, on the other hand, need to make a profit. At first glance, it seems that these two unchanging realities are in opposition. Some would argue that people cannot find meaning in organizations driven by a bottom-line perspective. Others would insist that productivity, as often as not, demands that the touchy-feely stuff be kept in check. Human beings may need to be appreciated and challenged, but that's not what business is all about. In a free-market system a business' first priority is to provide a return on investment. The needs of the employees must, at best, come second to profitability.

The premise of this book is that bottom-line reasoning simply misses the mark. For most people, their work is not just work. It is something of great importance. It is the purpose of their lives. And, as such, it is their work which most often defines the degree to which they will ever realize their intrinsic need to *matter*—to be valued, appreciated, challenged, and praised.

Organizational issues alone do not drive this need to *matter*. It is an egocentric leader who imagines that this dynamic is nothing more than an employee's desire to be *THE WINNER* of various political games which run amok in many organizations.

For most employees the need to *matter* is driven by forces which go unspoken but rarely unfelt. People work for what their efforts will bring to the people they love and care about. Their work sustains their families; buys their homes; puts food on the table; sends their kids to school; makes possible the happiness and rich memories of vacations, summer camps, ball games and holidays; and finally, allows them the dignity of a secure old age and burial.

These provide self-respect—they enable a person to affirm his or her intrinsic worth. These allow a man or a woman to experience the satisfaction of having "provided for my family." Their work is not just work. Their work is that which consumes the precious minutes and hours of their lives. That time, once spent, is gone forever. On one level or another, everyone knows this. People want the time they spend and the lives they live to matter.

The organization that can tap the energy, resourcefulness, and creativity of this *need to matter* will have empowered employees.

Empowered employees:

- are interdependent, not dependent.

- stay with a company because they want to, not because they have to.

- are loyal to mutually beneficial results, not to a legal entity.

- are focused on meeting the needs of others (customers, peers, employees, the organization) rather than worried about saving themselves.

- will openly and candidly share their ideas.

- are motivated to consistently perform at their best.

- find genuine ethical and philosophical (even spiritual) meaning in giving their best to a team which values their contribution.

This is what it means to *touch the magic of the human heart.* Not-for-profit organizations have understood this for decades. Have you ever noticed that some of the most poorly managed institutions (from a business, bottom-line perspective) go right on surviving, even thriving, year after year? Schools, churches, synagogues, universities, and various charities frequently go merrily on, even though their business practice would doom a for-profit organization. Have you ever wondered how this could be? These organizations survive because the people who are a part of them want them to survive. This is the magical power of the human heart. It is sweat and effort and energy, to be sure. More than that, it is the dogged determination a person brings to people and places where they know they matter.

Can you imagine the competitive advantage of an organization that successfully taps the magic of the human heart? Further, imagine such *heart* teamed with a sound business plan. Competitive advantage takes on a whole new meaning.

So where do leaders go to find the magic? Leaders go where people in all national, ethnic, or corporate cultures go to touch the magic. We go to fables and fairy tales.

Admittedly, this is an unsettling place for most business school trained, Hard-Knock U, bottom-line types to begin. Fables and fairy tales are about risk. Business is about minimizing risk and getting a good return on investment. Why, when you're orchestrating the music of a well-oiled machine (business), run the risk of letting some fool with a foghorn into the violin section? Why set up the delicate balance of people, production, and capital and then let a butcher with heavy thumbs mind the store?

Is it not more prudent (business-like) to be serious, rigid, controlling, respectable? No freedom, no empowered employees, no risk, no creativity; just a smooth, obedient machine presided over by an all-knowing and sober bank president with a gold watch. It just seems like good business.

That is, it seems like good business until you think about it and real-ize that risk, conflict, creativity, motivation, chaos, competitiveness, and profit are all cut from the same cloth: the magic of the human heart. These dynamics add up to good business. Messy as they are, they are part and parcel of human beings going about the business of busi-ness.

In order to get the best possible return on investment, an organiza-tion must get the best possible effort from its people. One without the other yields a declining return on investment and frustrated, demoti-vated employees.

Effective competitiveness means that an organization's people are candidly, assertively, and creatively interacting with one another. From a pool of well-advocated ideas, the single best idea will emerge. The trip, however, may look uncontrolled and chaotic. The risk can loom larger than the potential benefit. The whole thing can look like some-thing that couldn't possibly have a good ending. The fact is, engaging the human heart feels a lot like the telling and hearing of fables and fairy tales.

It may be that Walt Disney was the first motivational theorist to rec-ognize this strategy. At the very least, his creation of the job and title of "imagineer" is one of the best ever efforts to tap the resourcefulness of the human heart.

Disney understood that a business must turn a profit. He also understood the competitive spirit of an organization whose employees want to see it thrive. A business should not be just a place where a pay-check is issued, but a place where a person matters. Disney tapped the magic which comes from meeting an essential and perhaps the greatest human need: the need to be valued.

From the time we are small children, our fascination with fables and fairy tales is fueled by the need to matter. Fables and fairy tales are all about people and places where the honest efforts of a good person always prevail. We like these stories from our mother's lap onward because we know, no matter what others may say or insinuate, we are good persons with good intentions.

The phrase, *Once upon a time,* is more than the classic way to begin the spinning of a good yarn. It is a place where we go to remember what we are like at our best. A magical place is where people matter. If this magical place seems alien to business, it is business which has everything to gain by changing.

In the poorest work environment, employees punch clocks, meet schedules, and get the job done with *Once upon a time* waiting deep in their hearts. "One day the boss will ask my opinion...Someday I'll share this idea I've got...Surely the day will come when the company will notice me." *Once upon a time* is that time somewhere out there in a magical future, when the organization realizes; "I've got a heart I'd gladly give to a place where I matter."

A leader understands the magical "once upon a time" which resides in every human heart. A leader understands the magic of the human heart. A leader believes in what people are like at their best.

If you have reservations about the practical value of fables and fairy tales, try writing a fairy tale on the safe-and-sane view of business.

2

Leaders Honor Honest Mistakes

A leader is patient with people as they learn and grow.
Leaders treat others as they would like to be treated.

Once upon a time there was a princess who was under a curse. She was asleep and no one could wake her. The only way to break the curse was with an apple from the tree that grew in the middle of the garden at the western end of the world. What does the king do? Well, on the theory that a well-run, no risk operation makes the best of all possible worlds, he gets out his maps, briefs his generals, and sends a couple of well-supplied divisions to the garden to fetch the apple.

The whole thing is just a matter of getting an odd prescription from an inconveniently located drugstore that doesn't deliver. He uses his power, and the job is done. The apple is brought to the palace and applied to the princess. She wakes up; eats breakfast, lunch, and dinner forever after; and dies in bed at the respectable age of ninety-two.

Everyone knows, of course, that this is not the way to tell a good fairy tale. The story is too predictable. There's no magic. To begin with, the garden isn't on any of the maps. Only one man in the kingdom, the hundred-year-old Grand Geezer, knows where it is. When he is summoned, however, he asks to be excused. It seems that he is scheduled to die later that evening and therefore cannot make the trip. He happens to have a map, but there is a complication (isn't there always—if it's not one thing, it's another). The map has been drawn with magical ink and will be visible only to the right man for the job. The king, of course, inquires how this man is to be found. "Very simply," responds the Grand Geezer. "He will be recognizable by his ability to pat his head and rub his tummy at the same time, while whistling 'Puff the Magic Dragon.'"

The king calls in his nobles, all of whom are excellent musicians. They whistle, sing and chant (Gregorian) at the paper, but nothing appears. They do their darndest but have no luck. At last the king, in frustration, tells them to knock off for lunch and come back at two o'clock. Much too preoccupied to eat, the king strolls out onto the balcony and, lo and behold, what does he hear? Someone is walking down the road whistling 'Puff the Magic Dragon' while patting the top of his head and rubbing his tummy all at the same time.

It is, of course, the miller's son, a local high school dropout and village rowdy. The king, however, is not one to balk at ideologies when he needs help. He hauls the boy in, gives him the map, and packs him off with a bag of bagels (sourdough) and a bottle of Thunderbird. (Why waste good wine on an unsophisticated palate?)

That night the boy reads the map. It seems pretty straightforward, except for a warning at the bottom in block capitals: **AFTER ENTERING THE GARDEN GO STRAIGHT TO THE TREE, PICK THE APPLE AND GET OUT. DO NOT, UNDER ANY CIRCUMSTANCES, SPEAK TO THE THIRD PEACOCK ON THE RIGHT.**

Any child worth his Nintendo can write the rest of the story. The boy goes into the garden and gets as far as the third peacock on the right. The third peacock on the right startles him by asking, "Wouldn't you like a Butterfinger candy bar and a nice frosty mug of root beer?" Exhausted and parched from his long journey, the boy gobbles the candy bar and guzzles down the root beer. Before he knows it, he has fallen fast asleep. When he wakes up, he is in a pitch-black cave; a light flickers, a voice calls—and from there on all hell breaks loose. The boy follows an invisible guide with a cocked hat down rivers of fire in an

aluminum dinghy. He is imprisoned by the Crown Prince of the Sala-
manders. Finally he is rescued by a confused eagle (that looks a lot like
John Candy) who deposits him at the eastern end of the world.

The boy works his way back to the western end in the dead of win-
ter, gets the apple (having learned through trial and error not to speak
to the third peacock on the right), brings it home, touches it to the
princess' lips, awakens her, reveals himself to be the long-lost son of the
Eagle King, and marries the princess. Then, and only then, do they live
happily ever after.

It is the improbability and risk that make the story. There isn't a
child on earth who doesn't know the crucial moment—whose heart,
no matter how well he knows the story, doesn't skip a beat every time
the boy comes to the third peacock on the right. There is no one still in
possession of his humanity who doesn't recognize that moment as an
opportunity for the boy to prove that he matters despite his past mistakes. This is the second chance he's been hoping for, the chance to
prove he can get it right.

The safe universe may be a nice place to visit, but when a man or a
woman (i.e., employee) is looking for a chance to matter, he or she
instinctively knows not to go to the overstuffed bank presidents with
model worlds. Rather, they head straight to the same old disreputable
crowd their family has always done business with—the yarn spinners,
the chance givers, the risk takers—the leader who understands that
human nature is a bit chaotic. When you believe you matter the chaos
can quickly become superior performance. But first, employees must
believe they matter. This is the magic of the human heart. It is the
magic a person brings to people and places where that person knows an
individual's best efforts are valued.

The best leaders honor honest mistakes by allowing employees the
opportunity to recover from their mistakes. The best leaders are patient
with people as they learn and grow provided the employee demonstrates the capacity to learn from a mistake.

The best leaders treat others as they would like to be treated—the leader grants the employee a second chance.

3

Leaders Listen

A leader is supportive.
A leader voluntarily seeks to be helpful to others.

Once upon a time a young girl named Susan lived in a small town. It was the same town and the same street where Susan's mother, grandmother, and great-grandmother had all spent their girlhoods. As Susan grew from birth to young adulthood, her mother and grandmother gave her much advice about how to live and grow and do the right thing.

In particular, Susan's grandmother, whom Susan called Nannah, tried to guide her toward socially acceptable behavior. Nannah felt her guidance was particularly important since Susan seemed, at least to Nannah, a bit too interested in doing her own thing. Susan was not one to be guided by conventional ways of thinking and acting.

For example, although encouraged to play with dolls, Susan preferred mud pies and sand castles of her own special design. When scheduled for piano lessons, Susan never managed to arrive at her teacher's house on time; the neighborhood baseball game proved too much of a distraction. As other girls her age went through predictable phases and fascinations, Susan continued to march to her own drummer.

Finally, when Susan showed up for her seventeenth birthday party wearing cut-off jeans and a white T-shirt rather than the pretty cotton dress Nannah had bought for the occasion, it proved too much for Nannah. That afternoon Nannah reached the end of her patience. Nannah took Susan aside right then and there and scolded, *"Susan, why can't you be more like other girls your age? I swear, some day when you get to heaven, The Lord himself won't know what to do with you…but mark my word, He'll want to know why you weren't more like other girls."*

As it turned out, Nannah was not the only person who had reached the end of her patience that afternoon. Susan's response was quick and clear. In a voice easily as exasperated as Nannah's, Susan replied, *"Nannah, I think He'd be more alarmed if He had to ask, 'Why weren't you more like Susan?'"*

Susan is a test for her Nannah's patience. Susan is also her own person. Susan has the courage to assert her own value, even if it means disagreeing with her grandmother. Or, as the psychologist would say, Susan has a healthy sense of herself. Susan is self-confident.

If you're reaching for a dictionary let me save you the trip. Healthy self-confidence means that Susan (whether she would use these particular words or not) feels efficacious—adequate to meet life's challenges.

Or, stated another way, self-confidence is the reputation we get with ourselves. If that reputation is good, we feel good about ourselves. If it is not, we feel bad about ourselves. The consequences of that reputation carry over into our personal and professional relationships. For example, the degree to which we like ourselves is the degree to which we are free to like others. The degree to which we are comfortable with ourselves is the degree to which we are comfortable with others. The person in your workplace who has difficulty getting along with others is, most likely, having an even harder time getting along with himself. When I do not value me, it is difficult for me to value others. When I do not value me, I cannot value the organization.

So, does this mean that as long as Susan's self-confidence is high she and Nannah can have nothing but a frustrating relationship? No, that is not what it means. Susan and Nannah are like a two-person company with the same goal: They both want Susan to be happy, but they have competing ideas as to how to get there. Susan wants some say in her life. Nannah believes that, as the more experienced of the two, she knows best. All self-respecting employees want some say in their work. Bosses often believe their greater experience better qualifies them to structure an employee's work. Susan wants her thoughts and preferences considered. Nannah wants her grandmotherly instincts respected. Self-confident employees want their thoughts and preferences considered. Bosses tend to think that they know best because they are in charge.

Susan will be more open to her grandmother's hopes and dreams (goals) if she knows that her grandmother will consider her hopes and dreams (goals). Employees invariably bring higher motivation and commitment to the organization when they have been part of the goal-setting process. Emotionally healthy, self-confident employees want some say in both the goal and the path to the goal.

Interestingly enough, employees often set their goals higher than those goals that are set without the employees' input. People will stretch themselves but often resent being stretched by others. Susan, Nannah & Company, Inc. experience all the growing pains of any organization where people insist on being valued.

This is a good place to consider what Susan, Nannah & Company, Inc. can do to strengthen the self-confidence of every person in the organization. You may ask, "Why bother?" And the answer is that people who believe in themselves can be empowered. People who do not believe in themselves cannot be empowered. When I believe in me, and I know the organization believes in me, I think of work as my work. Here are seven suggestions for building employee self-confidence and setting the tone for empowerment.

1. **Be more concerned about making others feel good about themselves than in making them feel good about you or the organization.** Most people don't care what you think until they know you care. Until I know that my personal goals will be considered, the goals of the organization are just a means of getting a pay-

check and nothing more. It is a wise leader who realizes that one of the greatest unspoken fears we all have is that we will be accountable to someone who does not care about us. So the leader who does not treat employees with respect and consideration encourages employees to feel bad about themselves. This pushes employees toward a preoccupation with how to feel better about themselves. On the other hand, employees who are encouraged to feel good about themselves are free to focus on meeting the needs of others (i.e., customers, peers, and the needs of the organization).

2. **Encourage employees to view their work as a journey with many lessons to be learned.** Everyone is enrolled in a full-time, informal school called life. It does not have to be the school of hard-knocks. There is much to be learned (painlessly) by listening to lessons those who have been there can teach us. It is not in our best interest, or in the best interest of the organization, to spend precious time and energy reinventing the wheel.

On the other hand, it is also helpful to remember that people learn most willingly from persons they trust. Therefore, candid, full disclosure forms the foundation for corporate learning. Giving an employee a good performance review because the boss wants to avoid conflict is nothing short of setting the employee up to fail. Telling the boss what he or she wants to hear should not be rewarded. Telling the truth with compassion is a vital part of what it means to be a team player.

3. **Set employees free to try, to fail, to learn, and to move on.** Personal and organizational development is a process of trial, error, and experimentation. The faulty ideas are as much a part of the formula for success as the ideas that ultimately work. In such a setting people are not rewarded for merely making sure nothing goes wrong. They are rewarded for making a contribution. This means more than just doing a job. It means making a positive difference.

Here the foundation is loyalty: personal and organizational loyalty to employees who are making an informed, honest effort to make a difference! "Informed" means the employee has carefully thought about and worked through the idea prior to trying it out, including soliciting opinions and insights from others. "Honest effort" means the employee is acting in the best interest of the organization—not playing politics or attempting to cover up a prior mistake.

4. **Create a learning culture within the organization.** Refuse to allow learning to be something done at the occasional continuing education workshop. Have organizational leaders talk with employees about any newly acquired learning or skills. Reward people for demonstrating the acquisition of new skills. Provide frequent opportunities for employees to learn something new. Do not limit the learning opportunity to company business. Provide learning experiences which enhance the quality of the employees' life. For example, provide classes on personal financial management, retirement, or parenting. Remember, every time an employee makes the effort to learn something, he or she is practicing a skill which can only benefit the organization.

5. **Recognize and reward employees who maintain a positive attitude.** Personal attitude is a choice. Every person is responsible for how the choice he or she has made impacts others. No one is responsible for me but me. If I am willing to accept responsibility for my own life-view (attitude), it is a revealing indication that I will accept responsibility for myself in other areas as well.

The myth is that someone other than me is choosing my attitude for me. When another person is choosing my attitude (and this is never the case), it is often because I lack either the maturity or the courage (or both) to assert my right to choose how I will live and act. Such a perspective also flies in the face of mental health. We know that a core characteristic of mental health is the capacity to choose behavior. Therefore, if I want you to believe that I cannot choose to behave differently, in essence, I want you to believe that I am mentally ill.

No matter how smart or gifted an employee is, if his or her attitude is not constructive, it will affect the entire team. In most settings it takes time to build a can-do culture. Employees who choose not to have a constructive attitude will find it stressful to see constructive attitudes rewarded. Some will resist development of such a culture. Interestingly enough, the team members who have chosen to maintain a positive attitude will often deal very effectively with this resistance without the intervention of the team leader. Others will simply move on. Either way, over time what gets rewarded will get done and will become the norm.

Expecting others to be responsible for themselves is one of the more important ways of showing **respect** for another person. We protect small children. It is a given that they are too immature and naive to be held responsible for their attitude or actions. We feel much the same about the elderly who are senile. However, we are paying others a compliment (demonstrating respect) when we assume they are willing to be responsible for themselves. Such respect enhances the self-worth of individuals and teams. And healthy self-confidence builds a can-do culture.

6. **Ask at least one employee for his or her opinion each day—then be quiet and listen.** It could be argued that *listening* is the most effective motivational strategy a leader can practice. It is also the most neglected. Listening is personal. It builds mutual trust. It solicits the insights of those closest to the work being done.

Few people are naturally good listeners. Effective listeners acquire this skill by working at it. Recognizing that I may not be a good listener is the place to begin. Leaders will have to candidly critique their listening skills. As long as my listening skills go unexamined, I can tell myself "I listen well enough." It may be that I don't listen well enough. However, if I work at acquiring effective listening skills, I can.

Begin by asking questions like these: When others are talking, do I concentrate on what they are saying, or am I thinking about what I want to say when they finish? Do I ask questions about what others have said? Do I summarize what I've heard and test for understanding? The point is this, nothing changes until it becomes what it is. Until I believe I need to improve, I will see no need to make the effort.

One of the pitfalls of leadership is a pattern of thinking that others should be listening to me. I, on the other hand, should not have to waste time listening to others. After all, I'm the one with the knowledge, experience, and authority.

The higher you go in an organization, the less willing others are to risk your displeasure by asserting their right to be heard. Thus, they tell you what you want to hear or nothing at all. This is a precarious position for a leader. Leaders frequently fail because they make decisions based on poor or inadequate information. Ironically, in such instances, employees are often sitting on the very information the leader needs. When asked why they did not provide the information, their response is, "Nobody asked me"—which translates: "Nobody was listening."

The further you go in an organization, the more you must depend on others for accurate information.

Leaders who do not listen carefully and intelligently aren't going to get the facts they need, and people will resent their decisions: If you want to motivate me, listen to me. If you want me to believe that I am a valued member of the team, listen to me. If you want accurate and timely information, listen.

7. **Honor the uniqueness of each team member.** Finally, not only does Susan have a healthy sense of self-confidence, but at seventeen she already knows something about herself which every person feels and longs to have others recognize. Susan knows she is unique. Susan believes there is something special about her. Every person in every setting has an intuitive desire to have this recognized. If human beings share anything in common, it is the belief within ourselves that we are somehow special. It is the belief that there has never been anyone quite like us before, and there will never be anyone quite like us again. We are not just one in a million, we are the only one—the only one of us, at least.

The individual's need to feel special is met through family life and through the formation of personal relationships. No organization can ethically single out an individual as more special than others. We may even refer to our co-workers as family. However, a business, by its very nature, cannot be expected to meet an individual's need to feel special in the same way a family would.

What, then, does the idea of *honoring the uniqueness of each individual* have to do with the workplace? While a business cannot (and should not) seek to replace a family, an organization can *tap the energy of the unique contribution.* Every employee wants to feel that he or she contributes something special to the team. This does not mean encouraging employees to believe they are irreplaceable (that would simply be untrue). It does mean that as an effective team member, the individual is contributing something essential to the success of the team. If a team member is not contributing something essential to the team's success, why is the person on the team? Honoring the uniqueness of each individual means recognizing the something essential each person is contributing.

Typically, the recognition has to be as individual as the employee. With some, an occasional compliment is sufficient. With others, an award such as a plaque, a day off, a company jacket presented in the company of their peers is needed. It may be best to offer the reward in private as an employee may be harassed by peers because he or she was singled out. For still others, nothing short of increased wages or a bonus will do. Whatever the recognition, it must express appreciation for the individual's *unique contribution*. Then it will tap the *energy* we all bring to the people and places where we are special.

4

Leaders Model Courage and Consideration

A leader is trustworthy.
Leaders manage their own words and behavior.
A leader voluntarily self-corrects.

Once upon a time there lived a man named Bill. Bill owned a construction company which specialized in home building. Bill took great pride in the quality of the homes his company built. Bill used only the best materials and the most reliable methods. Bill spared no effort and cut no corners.

Bill was particularly proud of his crews. "The Best People Building the Best Homes" was his company motto. And, as far as Bill was concerned, his crews were just that—the best.

Carpenters, masons, plumbers, roofers, and electricians all knew their trade and took pride in their workmanship. For his part, Bill paid top wages and never failed to give his people the credit they deserved.

After many satisfying years of building homes, Bill began to think about retirement. As he thought about retiring, he thought about Pete. Pete was Bill's oldest and best foreman. When Bill retired, that's the day Pete had said he would hang it up, too.

Bill went to see Pete to tell him of his plans to retire. Bill told Pete he had one last job for him, "I'm headed out of town for about six months, Pete. While I'm gone I'd like you to take a crew out to that lot on Harvest Lane and build this house. Spare no reasonable expense. Make sure it is the kind of house in which a man would enjoy spending his retirement years." Bill then handed Pete a roll of plans and headed off on his trip.

Pete went to work. As he guided the crew through the initial phase of construction, he began to think about his future. "In all the years I've worked with Bill he's never been able to provide me with a retirement program. I've got social security and my savings. But will that be enough? Maybe it's time I started looking out for Pete."

In the following stages of construction Pete began to cut corners. Whenever he thought it would be difficult to detect, he used inferior materials. In other instances he replaced master craftsmen with inexperienced carpenters and masons, because they would accept lower wages. "Nobody'll know," Pete thought to himself. "I'll pocket the difference and be long gone by the time the shoddy construction is discovered."

In time, the house was completed. Bill returned from his trip. Seeing the house, Bill congratulated Pete on what Bill believed to be Pete's usual good work. Within a day or so, Bill asked Pete to meet him at the new house on Harvest Lane. At first, Pete was reluctant to go, "What if Bill has discovered the shoddy construction sooner rather than later?" Pete wondered to himself. Then Pete recalled how clever he had been in covering his tracks. "You'd have to live in that house for three or four years before it started falling apart," Pete reminded himself. "Bill couldn't possibly know this soon."

Pete headed on over to the new house on Harvest Lane, confident his deception would not be discovered. When Pete arrived, Bill was waiting on the large, airy front porch. Glancing at the house as he got out of the car, Pete thought to himself, "It is a beautiful house but not for long."

Bill greeted Pete with his usual warmth and immediately began telling him why he wanted Pete to meet him, "Pete, you've been a loyal friend and my best foreman for many years. I owe much of my success to you. I just couldn't retire without first letting you know how much I appreciate you. Here are the keys to the house. It is yours, lock, stock, and barrel. All I ask is that you live in it and enjoy it for the rest of your life."

As human beings we have an uncanny ability to act against our own best interest. Most of the time we recognize this inclination, and we control our impulses. Giving in to the urge to tell the boss where to go, or strangling the customer who used the blender we sold them to mix house paint and is now in our face demanding to know what they should do with it is not in our best interest. We can usually see temptations like these coming in time to put the brakes on what we'd really like to say.

At other times we are less perceptive. We commit selficide. Selficide occurs when I betray my best interest. It is acting against what is best for me. As a result, I usually end up destroying what I want most—to be seen as a person of integrity who can be trusted.

On one level, selficide is the failure to learn and grow from life's experiences. The failure to learn and grow means we make the same mistake more than once. It means that we teach others to think of us as persons who just can't quite get our act together. Or, worse, we unintentionally nurture the perception that we are not very smart. Such perceptions are not in our best interest. They constitute the committing of selficide.

On another level, selficide includes those momentary lapses when we forget that we have to live with the perceptions of others. We indulge ourselves, usually only for a moment (though it is often a moment long enough to get ourselves in trouble) in the fantasy of our self-sufficiency. We take a long, deep drag on our ego and imagine we can reach our goals without the support or cooperation of others. Our experience has taught us that no one succeeds for very long unless other people want us to succeed—and therefore invest in our success. Lost in the euphoria of our ego, we allow ourselves to forget. We forget that the cooperation of others is essential to our success. How others perceive us has a direct impact on our effectiveness.

The opposite of selficide is healthy self-interest. Pete's problem began when he confused self-interest with ego and committed selficide. Self-interest is not acting for self and against others. Healthy self-interest is good for us and for others. Self-interest is choosing long-term benefits over short-term gains.

We noted earlier that self-confidence is the reputation we get with ourselves. By contrast, integrity is the reputation we get with others. Bill's construction foreman, Pete, committed selficide the moment he decided he no longer needed Bill's trust. Personal integrity is a glass house each person builds and maintains over a lifetime. Our willingness to openly and reliably do the right thing by others determines how bulletproof the glass will be. Pete shot out his own windows. Or, to use another metaphor, Pete shot himself in the foot. In building a house he knew to be inferior, he was acting against his own best interest. As it turned out, it was a house he would have to live in. But, even if he did not live in it, he'd still have to live with the reputation of having built a sub-standard house.

The critical transition in Pete's thinking took place when he bought into the single greatest myth of the American workplace: I work for someone other than me.

The truth is, Pete never worked for Bill. All those years, Pete worked for Pete. Pete had always been self-employed. It just so happens that Bill was Pete's only customer. Everyone who works for a living is a company of one. Pete was never just Pete. He was always Pete, Inc.

As Pete, Inc., Pete has something important in common with all the other companies of one who are savvy enough to realize they are self-employed. Pete, Inc.; Lisa, Inc.; and Joe, Inc. all have destinies controlled by the same holding company, a holding company they may or may not know as Character Corp. Having their destinies controlled by Character Corp. means that their success is at the mercy of something more perilous than market forces.

Pete, Inc. is at the mercy of Pete's character. As a company of one, Pete's destiny is equal to, but never greater than, his personal integrity. If others find that Pete can be trusted, they'll keep doing business with him. If they discover that Pete cannot be trusted, they'll take their business elsewhere. Either way, the destiny of Pete, Inc. (what Pete does for a living) is controlled by the degree to which others experience him as trustworthy.

The most reliable way to keep Character Corp.'s stock up is to think of one's self as self-employed. My product is the value and trustworthiness of my character.

Here are the five benchmark questions you can use to evaluate how quality control is going in your company of one.

1. Is my vision of what I want my life (company of one) to be clearly defined?

2. Am I keeping my priorities straight?

3. Am I asking myself the difficult questions?

4. Am I overly concerned with image building?

5. Am I investing in the success of others?

1. Is my vision of what I want my life (company of one) to be clearly defined?

Most people offer a predictable response when asked, "What's your mission in life?" They will say they'd like to:

• be loved by their family.

• be thought of as a good person.

• abide by the golden rule.

- be remembered for having done something special

When pressed, however, most people do not have a conscious strategy for realizing their vision of what they'd like their life to be.

By contrast, a person of vision has a plan. Persons of vision have an idea how to get where they're going. That is not to say that every person or company of one must have an extensive Strategic Business Plan as one might find at AT&T or Wal-Mart. It does mean that a person of vision has a set of core principles which guides the course of his or her life. It is this clearly defined system of values against which all of life is judged that is the source of personal integrity.

As the source of personal integrity, a vision statement is the beginning of personal and organizational leadership. The vision statement will clearly identify the core principles by which I choose to live. It will provide overall direction. It will clarify my purpose and meaning. By referring to it and internalizing its meaning, I am more likely to choose behavior that serves my vision and reject behavior which does not. I am less likely to commit selficide.

An effective vision statement will provide answers to three essential questions:

- Do I matter?

- Where am I going?

- Who will go with me?

These three questions form the Chapman Paradigm (Illustrated below).

The Chapman Paradigm

1. Do I Matter?

3. Who will go with me?   2. Where am I going?

The first question is the esteem question: "Do I matter?" Self-esteem is the critical starting point for effective personal and public leadership. The degree to which I value "me" is the degree to which I am free to value others. The degree to which I value others is the degree to which I can build mutually beneficial relationships. This dynamic is illustrated by The Courage-Consideration Continuum shown on the following page.

The vertical axis of the continuum registers the degree to which I have the courage to advocate the value of my convictions. Through advocacy I affirm that I am a person of worth and value. As a person of worth, I have something of value to contribute to the human experience. By asserting the value of what I have to offer, I maintain my self-esteem.

The Courage-Consideration Continuum

Assertiveness, however, is only the first step. I must demonstrate that I will be responsible for myself. This means honoring my commitments and accepting the consequences of my decisions—whether those consequences are good or bad. In this, I build and sustain a strong sense of self-worth and, therefore, feel efficacious, adequate to life and equal to the task of living as an adult among other adults.

Why do I feel hurt and confused when my courage fails me? Typically, this inadequacy happens when a person says or does something which leaves me feeling discounted, abused, mistreated, or wronged. If I fail to stop the abuse, fail to insist that the mistreatment be corrected, or fail to demand that the wrong be righted, my courage has failed me—and my sense of adequacy will suffer.

By failing to assert my value, I feel on the inside like I've affirmed the discounting. If I allow another to discount me long enough, the feelings of inadequacy will move from my inside to my outside. When on the outside, others will begin to experience me as having either an inferiority or a superiority complex. Feelings of both inferiority and superiority are driven by feelings of inadequacy. Inferiority is the "I'm less than human" response to being discounted. Superiority is the "I'm more than human—superman" response to being discounted.

By refusing to be discounted, I assert my self-worth. I answer "YES" to the question: "Do I matter?" In mustering the courage to assert my intrinsic value, I position myself to lead myself and others. Therefore, courage is the most essential virtue because it assures that all other virtues will be advocated.

The Courage-Consideration Continuum

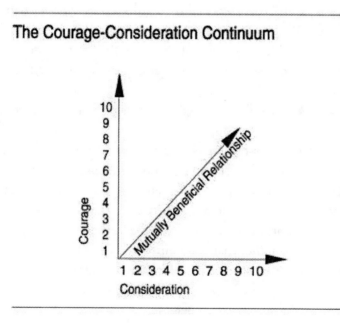

The horizontal axis of the continuum registers the degree to which I have consideration for the value of others. Consideration, in this context, is like the opposite side of the same coin. On one side is the courage to assert my values. On the other side is the consideration which allows others to assert their value. Consideration is willingly granting to others what we demand for ourselves—to be treated as persons of worth.

Consideration cannot be conditional. It must be granted whether the other person likes or dislikes me; treats me well or treats me poorly; affirms my value or discounts me. As long as I choose to interact with a person, I must grant him or her consideration. When and if the time comes when I feel I can no longer grant an individual consideration, we both then need to go our separate ways.

Consideration is a measure of my strength of character. It is driven by my value system, not by the value system of another. Otherwise, the consideration I extend to others will be nothing more than a tit-for-tat reaction to the behavior of others. My courageous self-confidence does not allow the inconsideration of another to regulate my consideration. I treat others with consideration because it is the core of who I am and what I am about. I am a person of courage and consideration. I will assert my value and I will respect the right of others to assert their value.

If either axis of the courage-consideration continuum is uneven, the relationship will eventually cease to be mutually beneficial. If the vertical (courage) is significantly weaker than the horizontal (consideration), I may well become little more than a doormat for others. If the horizontal (consideration) is weaker than the vertical (courage), I risk discounting others whether that is my intention or not.

The key is a proactive balance. In taking the initiative, I can work to keep each axis strong and balanced. I want strong vertical and horizontal axes because I want others to experience me as a person of both courage and consideration. Such a balance responsibly asserts my worth and respects the worth of others. Such a dynamic is mutually beneficial. A dynamic balance is an excellent place from which to lead.

The second question raised and answered by an effective vision statement is the question of goals and standards.

When I ask, "Where am I going?" I am establishing a direction and a benchmark. I am consciously choosing a path to a destination. In addition, I am establishing a standard for measuring progress toward a goal and the degree to which I maintain personal values in the process. I am not interested in merely traveling from point A to point B but in making the trip to my goals with my value system intact.

Let's say, for example, that after much thought and consideration I settle on a personal vision statement. I determine that vision to be as follows:

• I will tell the truth with compassion.

• I will live my own life.

• I will be loyal to my family, friends, and associates.

In addition, let's say that as a front-line leader I decide, after consultation with the leadership of my company, that I'd like to be a department manager someday. Becoming a department manager is my goal, a vital first half of the answer to the question "Where am I going?"

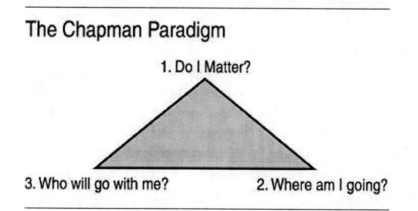

The Chapman Paradigm

1. Do I Matter?

3. Who will go with me?   2. Where am I going?

The other half of the answer is the benchmark. In this example, the benchmark is my commitment to truth telling, self-worth, and loyalty.

As I move toward the realization of my goal (becoming a department manager), I am concerned with more than the clever and the expedient. I want each action step to take me closer to my goal, and I want every action step to be consistent with my personal standards. Thus, when I evaluate my progress I ask not only the geographic question "How far have I come?" but also the standard question "Have I kept faith with my vision?" If I have been truthful and compassionate, the answer is yes. If I have refused to allow others to discount me, my answer is yes. And, if I have remained loyal to the best interest of family, friends and associates, my final answer is yes.

Maintaining a strong link between my goals and my standards assures the vitality of my personal integrity. Others will experience me as a person who can be trusted. My capacity to lead others will be enhanced. My stock will hold its value. My company of one will remain competitive. My character will continue to be a viable corporation.

The third and final question of a vision statement is the relational question, "Who will go with me?" Here my response builds on the answers for questions one and two. Asserting one's personal worth (Do I matter?) will have a direct impact on relationships. Being committed to a set of values (Where am I going?) will affect how others experience me.

The consequences will follow one of two paths. There will be those who will respect me for asserting my personal worth and being faithful to my values. They will be interested in associating with me if they find me to be a person of courage and consideration. They know I not only have the courage to be my own person, but I also have the consideration to allow another to be his or her own person as well.

On the other hand, a healthy sense of self-worth and integrity may make others uncomfortable. They may be so uncomfortable that they will be unable or unwilling to go with me. They may feel that my commitment to truth telling is naive. My self-confidence may seem threatening. They may consider my loyalty to family, friends, and associates an unnecessary nuisance. Any one, or all, of these commitments may make me someone they don't care to move through the years with.

The truly tough part of personal integrity is getting used to people moving in and out of our lives. We meet someone at a P.T.A. meeting or at the office and gradually become hopeful that the person will become a treasured friend and associate. Then, much to our disappointment, we discover that the individual finds our principles unsettling. They see nothing wrong with a little dishonesty, particularly if it gets them what they want. They don't mind being discounted, as long as it keeps them on the winning side of office politics. And, as for loyalty, it is for the naive and foolish. Gradually, they choose a course different from the one we are committed to. They exit our life. We, in turn, make the necessary but painful choice of principle over friendship.

Along with personal satisfaction, disappointment also comes with our vision. Occasionally, commitment to our principles will lead us to move through a period of time or a task alone. It is not that no one else on the planet shares our commitment to honesty, self-worth, or loyalty. The most principled person does not have a monopoly on ethical behavior. However, those who share our principles may not happen (by no design of their own) to be available. It is in keeping faith with our principles at such times that we are assured of being once again joined by others who share our principles.

If getting used to people moving in and out of our lives is the toughest part of integrity, then being unable to explain ourselves when appropriate is the most frustrating. Just as personal integrity can mean loneliness, it can also mean doing the right thing even when we cannot explain.

Sometimes the inability to explain has to do with the person to whom we are offering the explanation. It may be that the person has no context for understanding what we're talking about. The individual may be a person of integrity with a value system radically different from ours. Or, the person may simply be unprincipled, and the idea of doing the right thing may hold no interest. In such instances it is important to test our motives to make sure we are not being condescending or self-serving in our assessment of the other person.

At other times, doing the right thing may defy explanation. We cannot qualify why something is wrong for us, but in our heart, we know it is. While this has an emotional dynamic, it is also pragmatic. More often than not, we don't get to choose between the clearly wrong and the clearly right. We have to work in gray areas where a judgment call is required. Winning the respect of others when we choose what is clearly right will enable others to trust us when we have to work in the gray areas. Either way, choosing a principled course of action cannot be subject to our ability to explain. Doing the right thing even when we cannot explain just comes with the turf. Such instances not only measure a person's commitment to his principles, they also prepare a person to lead.

Clearly defining my vision of my company of one allows me to focus on balancing my priorities, the second benchmark.

2. Am I keeping my priorities straight?

The second benchmark question for our company of one is the special relationship between balance and productivity. Deciding what is important and disciplining oneself to focus on what is important are essential to success.

Unfortunately, priorities have a tendency to get shuffled when we're not paying attention. The urgent pushes the important aside. With dozens of fires to put out, what really matters gets lost in the rush. The resulting scenario is predictable. A leader works hard, makes personal sacrifices, gets the job done, and becomes successful. And then, when it is too late, the leader discovers the enormous price of success: the marriage is in shambles, the children are strangers, and physical health is endangered. The resulting disappointment is not what the leader had in mind. Success was supposed to be much sweeter.

What happened? The leader, perhaps unintentionally, bought into the myth that success in one area of life assures happiness in all areas of life. Any life which has a single focus is unbalanced. The unbalanced life is a personal disaster waiting to happen. It may take twenty-five years for the harm to become evident. It may take only five years. This much we know: A leader who proactively seeks to live a balanced life is more productive over a longer period of time. By contrast the leader with a single focus, such as a workaholic, is three times as likely to experience burnout. The leader who focuses all of his or her energy on succeeding at the office may rise quickly but is also likely to fail sooner than the leader who seeks balance.

The key to long-term success is productivity driven by personal balance. Most of us want to succeed in every important area of our life. We want to experience professional success. But we also want to achieve personal, physical, mental, social, and ethical success.

The Life Wheel

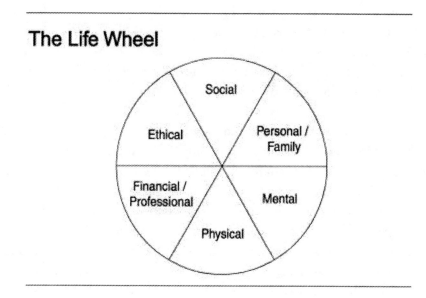

Here it may be helpful to think of success as a wheel. The wheel has six compartments, all connected and in one way or another dependent on each other. If each compartment is properly inflated and receives appropriate attention, the wheel will roll smoothly. If any compartment is over or under inflated, the ride will be bumpy.

By giving appropriate attention to each of the six areas, the leader is equipped with two potent advantages for long-term success: personal resilience and the capacity for self renewal.

Resilience is achieved by drawing one's emotional support from more than one source. If I'm experiencing success in all six areas of the wheel, then I can more easily bounce back from disappointment. If I have a bad day at work I can gain emotional renewal from going home or socializing with a good friend. But, if my work is my life, disappointment at work leaves me with no place to go for renewal. In time, my resilience—the capacity to recover from disappointment—is weakened. Thus, my ability to renew myself is depleted. Once my emotional resources are depleted, burnout is inevitable.

Does burnout mean it's over for me? No, many burned-out leaders recognize what's happened to them and begin the difficult process of properly inflating their wheel. Leaders do recover from burnout. The collapse of personal relationships and the loss of many productive years make burnout worth avoiding.

3. Am I asking myself the difficult questions?

The third benchmark question deals with my capacity to self-critique. It focuses on my ability to objectively evaluate my motives and actions. Quality control in my company of one requires that I self-critique prior to my critique of others. The questions I ask others I must ask myself. Effective leadership assures accountability. Principle-centered leadership makes sure that accountability begins with the leader.

When I ask myself the difficult questions, I self-critique my fitness to lead. If I fail to self-critique, my motives may appear to be self-serving. Once my motives become suspect, I risk losing the moral authority to ask others to do the right thing. Once I no longer have the right to ask others to do the right thing, my effectiveness as a leader is diminished, if not lost. By asking myself the difficult questions, I position myself to be effective.

I self-critique by thinking through my words and behavior:

- Have I said something I should not have said?

- Have I failed to say something I should have said?

- Have I done something I should not have done?

- Have I failed to do something I should have done?

I self-critique by thinking through my relationship to the organization:

- Why am I doing this?

- Who will be affected?

- How should it be done?

- When should it be done?

Why am I doing this? Am I doing this for the right reasons? Do I have the right motives? Is there an inappropriate personal agenda in my plans? Is it the right thing to do?

Who will be affected? Will anyone be harmed? Is the harm unavoidable? Have steps been taken to assure the harm is minimized? Have explanations been provided? Have questions been answered? Has open, candid communication been encouraged?

How should it be done? Have I carefully considered alternatives? Have I included others in the decision making process? What is the result I am looking for? Does the chosen course of action have the best chance of moving us toward the desired results?

When should it be done? Is this the right time? Is there a more appropriate time? Am I trading long-term results for a short-term advantage? Is the timetable realistic? Is the timetable mutually acceptable to the key players? Does the timetable allow for the unexpected?

4. Am I overly concerned with image building?

Benchmark question number four notes the difference between show business and substance. Integrity, by definition, is genuine. Character is not an image fabricated to manipulate others.

Madison Avenue has taught us that we must package ourselves in order to sell ourselves. Although attention should be paid to putting our best foot forward, character's focus is on relaying reality, not selling an act. Presenting myself as something other than what I am raises questions about my trustworthiness. Posturing may cause others to view my motives as bogus. Invariably, the value of my stock will go down.

Presenting a good professional image is an asset. Valid principle-centered leadership, however, does not depend on wearing designer fashions or knowing when to use the salad fork. The focus of integrity is on building a reputation, not merely projecting an image. Like principle-centered leadership, true professionalism includes a dogged commitment to the truth and seeing things for what they are.

Here are some questions which will assist a leader in gauging preoccupation with image building.

How good am I at telling myself the truth? Truth telling is an ethical concept which refers to the capacity to be loyal to the truth and the spirit of the truth. This raises the bar for honesty. It is not enough to merely refuse to lie. I must insist on never using the truth to suggest what is false either implicitly or explicitly. Implicitly, I can use the truth to suggest what is false by withholding information or by twisting the truth to create a false impression.

Explicitly, I can use the truth to suggest what is false by embellishing the truth. I can suggest something is more serious or less serious than it actually is by tone of voice or the words I choose. For example, for most of us the biggest personal barrier to telling ourselves the truth is cognitive dissonance. Cognitive dissonance is the capacity to lie to ourselves convincingly. We are all tempted by cognitive dissonance. Anytime someone tells us something unpleasant, it is tempting to rationalize or to engage in denial. We all want to be emotionally comfortable. Sometimes we want it badly enough to lie to ourselves.

Do I make decisions based on what is right or on what is most easily accepted? Do I have to take a poll before I can candidly relay information? Does opposition, even when it is self-serving, cause me to retreat? Do I shelve my convictions at the first sign of conflict? Am I committed to doing what I believe is best or is it more important to me to be liked?

Do I change my personality, speech, or actions according to the people I am with? Every healthy personality includes a desire to be liked. No one wants others to groan when we enter the room. We would like others to like us. But being a people-pleaser is an unacceptable price for being liked. Being liked does not have the same value as being trusted. Ideally, it is good to be both liked and trusted. But when a choice has to be made, it is personal integrity that secures the value of our stock. This does not mean that I am free to act like a bull in a china shop as long as I'm candid. The consideration axis of the courage-consideration continuum (page 27) requires me to treat others with courtesy. A lack of compassion in truth-telling is just another form of posturing.

Do I hog the credit when things go well and find someone to blame when things do not go well? Peers and employees usually find this kind of behavior unsettling. It de-motivates the team and strains relationships with the selection of each scapegoat. The most effective teams are bound together by mutual respect. Sharing the credit for success builds trust. Accepting responsibility for failure does even more to build trust. People instinctively know it takes less character to handle success than to overcome failure; the leader who will own his mistakes is a leader they want to see succeed. The leader who postures at the expense of others is a leader they would like to see fail.

5. Am I investing in the success of others?

The fifth and final benchmark question emphasizes the value of win-win relationships. In the story about the construction foreman, Pete attempts to construct a win-lose relationship. He assumes he can establish a long-term scenario in which he is the only winner. This is almost never the case. Long-term success is almost always the result of win-win partnerships built through years of cooperative effort.

Investing in the success of another speaks to the deepest needs and interests of the people around us. Everyone wants to experience some measure of success. Everyone believes individuals have a right to benefit from their efforts. Effective leadership takes these needs and interests into account. This sensitivity is not mushy or patronizing. It recognizes that it is unethical and self-defeating to treat others as a means to an end. People do what they do for their own reasons. Those reasons, more often than not, fit the vision a person has for his or her life. A principled leader respects that vision and works to build win-win relationships. Relationships which sustain long-term motivation and commitment are mutually beneficial.

Some of the more notable roadblocks to win-win relationships include pride, moodiness, perfectionism, oversensitivity, and negativism.

Win-win relationships rarely develop when others are treated as inferior. Most people find it difficult to accept a snobbish or know-it-all attitude. Few people view being discounted as an investment in their success.

Moodiness is an immature characteristic detrimental to personal relationships. Moody people tend to be fickle. Fickle individuals are perceived to be unreliable.

Perfectionism is an obsessive need to perform flawlessly. It stifles creativity and turns people away. Perfectionists can rarely affirm themselves; therefore, it's difficult for them to affirm others.

Oversensitive people are constantly licking their wounds. They look inward and are not aware of others. Naturally, it is hard to believe they care about the success of others.

Negativism poses the greatest threat to win-win relationships. It could even be said that negativism energizes all the other road blocks listed above. Negative people typically do not attract positive people. Positive persons know there is nothing mutually beneficial about naysayers.

On a practical level, here are some reliable suggestions for investing in the success of others.

Be patient.
As long as there is good reason to believe people are doing their best, cut them some slack. If a person is unable to do the job, tell him or her. As long as an individual is making acceptable progress, offer encouragement.

Be familiar with the problems of others.
Do your best to relate on a firsthand basis. Don't assume you know what there is to know because you came up through the ranks. Keep your knowledge and experience fresh. People must be able to trust you on the basis of today's facts, not on yesterday's experience alone.

Assure others of your confidence in them.
When an associate does a good job, tell him or her. When an employee improves performance, let him or her know. If team members express doubt about their ability to master a new process, bolster their confidence. Look for opportunities to let those who have earned your confidence know you believe in them.

Take care to give others credit for their efforts and their ideas.
Investing in others means allowing them to keep what is rightfully theirs. Most of us understand this as it applies to personal property. We certainly would not take anyone's car keys from their desk without permission and treat their car as if it were our own. Ethically speaking, a person's ideas and efforts fall under the same guideline. Every team member deserves to benefit from original ideas. Team members have a right to expect credit for their efforts. Leaders can stand on their own initiative. They do not steal the ideas or manipulate the behavior of others.

In our opening story, Pete committed the most fundamental mistake a leader can make—he failed to lead himself. The consequence of his failure to manage his own words and behavior was selficide. Principled leaders do not commit selficide. They are admired for the courage with which they self-correct and the consideration with which they relate to others. As a result, such a leader reaps the ever-increasing benefits of trust and respect.

5

Leaders Value Integrity

A leader is loyal to the best interest of the common good.
A leader is guided by an abiding faith in right.

Once upon a time there lived a man named Henry "Hank" Bedford Bannister, Jr. On February 19, 1996, Hank traveled to Yale to deliver the first of the Bannister Leadership Lectures that had been established in memory of his father. More than forty years earlier, Henry Bedford Bannister, Sr., had established Bannister Furniture Limited. Now president and CEO of Bannister Furniture Limited, Hank, as his father's successor, led a company widely respected as a good corporate citizen. It was a great place to work. It was a place where associates (employees) when asked, "Where do you work?" were proud to respond, "B.F.L."

That day in February Hank had endured a bad trip. The flight from Chattanooga to Hartford, with a connection through Nashville, had been delayed. Arriving in New Haven after midnight, Hank was exhausted from a long day and very little sleep the night before. He ordered dinner, ate, and then lay down to sleep without bothering to undress. About five o'clock the next morning Hank got up and began to shave. Hank still had not been able to formulate a plan for the lecture he was to present at 9:00. Procrastination had always been his number one developmental need, all the way back to the time he worked as an entry level clerk on the loading dock when his father had run the company. Somehow, he always came through in a pinch. Yet, he had come to New Haven without so much as a note card. He assumed it would all come to him somewhere between lift-off in Chattanooga and the podium in New Haven.

Just as he had his face lathered and was searching for his razor, the whole speech came to him out of nowhere. He dropped his razor and grabbed a pencil, dashing off the outline. As Hank distractedly returned to his razor, he cut himself badly. That cut was a hint of things to come.

Bannister Furniture Ltd. was more than a good corporate citizen and a great place to work. It was an ideal, a model for other corporations. It was a model led by honest, principled men and women with a vision. At the top of that model and at the center of that vision had always been the Bannister family. Henry, Sr., had gained national and international renown as the principled-centered leader of a new entrepreneurial age. After all, it was Henry's pristine business ethics which had brought Hank to New Haven. Yale was the alma mater of both Henry, Sr., and Hank. An endowment provided for The Henry Bedford Bannister, Sr., Chair in Principle-Centered Leadership. Business leaders and academics who admired the high ethical standards Henry, Sr., had brought to the competitive arena established the chair. Henry had demonstrated, once and for all, that an entrepreneur could turn a good profit while doing the right thing.

Now the leadership of B.F.L. and its prized reputation had fallen on Hank's shoulders. It was a role he had prepared for all his life. It was an honor and a challenge he gladly embraced some seven years earlier at his father's death. Like his father before him, Hank knew how to do the right thing. But somewhere between the knowing and the doing, the right thing had gotten lost in a price-fixing scheme. He had gotten sucked into a dubious competitive strategy and then had stayed long after he discovered it to be an illegal scam. The rumors about the scheme were no longer whispers but now were beginning to appear in print as incriminating internal memos were being leaked. Some people were taking sides; others were running for cover. The feds were formulating criminal anti-trust charges, and a public trial was not far in the future.

Hank's reputation and career were in danger, but much more was at stake. It was, in some measure, Bannister Furniture Ltd. It was everything Henry, Sr., believed in and stood for and what Hank had come to Yale to talk about.

So when Hank stood there looking into the hotel mirror with soap on his face and a razor in his hand, part of the reflection he saw was his own shame and disappointment. He could blame no one but himself for breaching his father's business ethic. A religious man, Hank saw in the mirror a judgment even more difficult to bear than God's: his own judgment of himself. When Hank had difficulty forgiving himself for disappointing his father, he remembered the words his father often spoke, "God is merciful, but none of us are very good at showing mercy for ourselves." That morning in New Haven, Hank felt no mercy, only shame.

Hank found himself casting his mind back across the years like the whip of a fly rod. Hanging in mid-air like a perfect trout lure just before it lands in the water was Henry's Code of Ethics. This document was in every lobby and office of Bannister Furniture Ltd. Principled, focused, and straightforward describe the perfect simplicity of the Bannister Ethic. Hank had known the code as long as he had known his ABC's.

The Code of Ethics was three direct questions:

Is it legal?

- Will I be violating either civil law or company policy?

Is it balanced?

- Is it fair to all concerned in the short term as well as the long term?

- Does it promote win-win relationships?

How will it make me feel about myself?

- Will it make me proud?

- Would I feel good if my family knew about it?

- Would I feel good if my decision was published in the newspaper?

For the first time since becoming company president and CEO, Hank realized his answers were now the wrong answers. Yes, he had broken the law and company policy. No, what he had done was not fair to anyone, and he felt neither pride nor pleasure at the prospect of his family and community finding out what he had done.

Standing there in the early morning twilight with his face lathered and bleeding, Hank asked himself the question men always ask when they discover a self-inflicted wound: *How could this have happened?*

The wound was self-inflicted, to be sure. It was also wrapped in self-pity. His reasoning had followed a predictable pattern. Hank winced when he thought how convincingly he had lied to himself. "To lie to one's self and believe the lie are the most cowardly things men do," would have been his father's assessment. Those who knew Hank's father and his homespun wisdom would have admiringly called this a "Henryism." Many "Henryisms" were beginning to return to Hank's memory as he pondered how it had all unfolded.

B.F.L. had always nestled in the mountain valley sixty miles northeast of Chattanooga. There, the Great Smoky Mountains gave B.F.L. a warm feeling factories usually lack. Bethlehem was the town's name. It had been founded around the turn of the century by a hearty band of Pennsylvania Amish. Unhappy with things up North, they had come South to this mountain valley. The "Andy Griffith Show" could have been filmed in Bethlehem with no need to add a single prop. Tree-lined streets; modest, neatly kept homes with wide front porches; steepled churches; a gazebo park at the center; and even the requisite town drunk graced the town of Bethlehem.

He was no Otis, but he made everyone feel better. His name was Morgan although most folks referred to him with a holier than thou air as "that drunk." Yet Henry, Sr., had been one of the few respectable people who would stop and pass the time of day with Morgan. When they happened to see Morgan, Henry liked to tell Hank, "People worth looking up to don't need anybody to look down on." And Hank had learned that lesson.

Even so, the Amish were still around and gave Bethlehem that final, sweet touch of quaintness with their horse-drawn buggies and black, Sunday-go-to-meetin' frock coats. Their handmade quilts drew tourists and tourists' dollars. The real money, however, was at B.F.L. Bethlehem held three thousand souls in her hands. Of these, four hundred ten won their daily bread at Bannister Furniture. Another dozen businesses gather B.F.L. table scraps, the kind small suppliers often glean from a larger customer's profits.

To say the least, B.F.L. was the economic soul of Bethlehem; B.F.L. and Bethlehem were interchangeable. B.F.L. was Bethlehem Furniture, and Bethlehem was Bannistertown.

Hank sat down on the bed in his hotel room. He thought to himself, "Suddenly, I feel tired. Maybe drained is a better word." Wearily Hank wiped the shaving cream from his face. Looking at the towel as it wiped away the mix of soap and blood, Hank's mind drifted back to when things had begun to go wrong...

Hank's dilemma is all too familiar. It raises the oldest ethical question: Why do good leaders make bad ethical decisions? Is it because these men and women who otherwise appear to be good people are in fact immoral? Such a question defies any common sense answer. The truth, I think, is less glamorous and less satisfying for those who like to use the actions of a few misbegotten souls to explain evil. Hank and his associates are ordinary men and women not very different from you or me. They found themselves in a dilemma, and they solved it in a way that seemed the least troublesome: *They decided not to disclose information which might hamper sales*. The consequences of their decision—both to the public and ultimately to B.F.L.—did not fully occur to them at the time.

The Bannister Furniture case illustrates the fine line between acceptable and unacceptable managerial behavior. Leaders are expected to strike a difficult balance—to pursue their companies' best interests, but not overstep the bounds of what outsiders will tolerate. Even the best leaders can find themselves in a bind and not know how far is too far. In retrospect, they can usually tell where they should have drawn the line, but no one manages in retrospect. We can only live and act today and hope that whoever looks back on what we did will judge that we struck the proper balance.

In a few years, many of us may be found delinquent for decisions we are making now about tobacco, clean air, and the use of some other seemingly benign substances. The leaders at Bannister Furniture may have believed that they were acting in the company's best interest, that what they were doing would never be found out, or even that it wasn't really wrong. These rationalizations endangered the company and contributed to its downfall.

Why do leaders do things that ultimately inflict great harm on their companies, themselves, and those whose patronage the organization depends? Although the particulars may vary, the motivating beliefs are much the same. Here we're examining them in the context of the corporation, but we know that these feelings are basic throughout society. We find them wherever we go because we take them with us.

When we look more closely at the Bannister Furniture case, we can delineate four commonly held rationalizations that can lead to misconduct. (1) A belief that the activity is within reasonable ethical and legal limits, that is, not really illegal or immoral. (2) A belief that the activity is in the individual's or the corporation's best interest, that the individual would somehow be expected to undertake the activity. (3) A belief that the activity is safe because it will never be found out or publicized, the classic crime and punishment issue of discovery. (4) And finally, a belief that because the activity helps the company, the company will condone it and even protect the person who engages in it.

Rationalization One:
The conduct is not really illegal or immoral.

The idea that an action is not really wrong is an old issue. How far is too far? Exactly where is the line between smart and too smart? Between sharp and shaded? Between profit maximization and illegal conduct? The issue can be complex. It involves an interplay between top management's goals and middle managers' effort to interpret those aims. Put enough people in an ambiguous, ill-defined situation and some will conclude that whatever hasn't been labeled specifically wrong must be okay, especially if there are rewards for certain acts. Top executives seldom ask their direct reports to do things that are against the law or are imprudent. But organizational leaders sometimes leave things unsaid or give the impression that there are things they don't want to know about. In other words, whether deliberately or otherwise, they seem to distance themselves from their reports' tactical decisions in order to keep their own hands clean if things go awry. Often they lure ambitious lower-level leaders by implying that rich rewards await those who can produce certain results and that the methods for achieving them will not be examined too closely.

How can leaders avoid crossing a line that is seldom precise? Unfortunately, most know that they have overstepped it only when they have gone too far. They have no reliable guidelines about what will be overlooked or tolerated and what will be condemned or attacked. When leaders must operate in murky borderlands, the most reliable guideline is an old principle—*when in doubt, don't.* That may seem like a timid way to run a business. One can argue that if this principle actually took hold among middle managers who run most companies, it might take the enterprise out of free enterprise. But there is a difference between taking a worth-while economic risk and risking an illegal or immoral act to make a few extra dollars. The difference between becoming a success and becoming a statistic lies in knowledge, including self-knowledge, not daring. Contrary to popular belief, leaders are not paid to take risks, they are paid to know which risks are worth taking. Also, maximizing profits is the company's second priority, not its first. The first is insuring its survival. Any leader can be tempted to take an inappropriate risk because of their companies' demands. But the same superiors who press you to do more and to do it better or faster or less expensively will turn on you should you cross the fuzzy line between right and wrong. They will blame you for exceeding instructions or for ignoring their warnings. The smartest managers already know that the best answer to the question, "How far is too far?" is "Don't try to find out."

Rationalization Two:
The activity is in the individual's or the corporation's best interest; the individual would somehow be expected to undertake the activity.

Believing that unethical conduct is in the person or corporation's best interest nearly always results from a parochial view of those interests. For example, Alpha Industries, a Massachusetts manufacturer of microwave equipment, paid $57,000 to a Rathion manager, ostensibly for a marketing report. The Air Force investigators charged that the report was a ruse to cover a bribe. Alpha wanted some contracts that the Rathion manager supervised. Those contracts ultimately cost Alpha a lot more than the amount paid for the report. After the company was indicted for bribery, its contract was suspended and its profits promptly vanished. Alpha isn't unique in this transgression. In 1984, the Pentagon suspended 453 companies for violating procurement regulations. Ambitious managers look for ways to attract favorable attention and to distinguish themselves from their peers. They do whatever will make them look good in the short run while ignoring the long-term implications. They skimp on maintenance or training or customer service, and they get away with it for a while. The sad truth is that many managers have been promoted on the basis of great results obtained in just those ways, leaving unfortunate successors to inherit the inevitable whirlwind. The problems they create are not always traced back to them. Organizations cannot afford to be hoodwinked in this way. They must be concerned with more than just results; they must look very hard at how results are obtained.

Rationalization Three:
The activity is safe because it will never be found out or publicized, the classic crime and punishment issue of discovery.

Believing that one can probably get away with irresponsible risk-taking is perhaps the most difficult rationalization to deal with because it's often true. A great deal of prescribed behavior escapes detection. We know that conscience alone does not deter everyone. For example, First National Bank of Boston pleaded guilty to laundering satchels of twenty dollar bills worth one-point-three billion dollars. Thousands of satchels must have passed through the bank's doors without incident before the scheme was detected. That kind of heavy, unnoticed traffic breeds complacency. How can we deter wrongdoing that is unlikely to be detected? We can make it more likely to be detected. Today's discovery process allows a plaintiff's attorneys to comb through a company's records for incriminating evidence. Had this process been in place when Johns-Manville concealed evidence on asbestosis, there probably would have been no cover-up. Mindful of the likelihood of detection, Johns-Manville might have chosen a different course and could very well be thriving today without the protection of the bankruptcy courts.

The most effective deterrent is not to increase the severity of punishment for those caught, but to heighten the perceived probability of being caught in the first place. For example, police have found that parking an empty patrol car at locations where motorists often exceed the speed limit reduces the frequency of speeding. Neighborhood crime watch signs decrease burglaries. Simply increasing the frequency of audits and spot checks is a deterrent, especially when combined with three other simple techniques—scheduling audits irregularly, making at least half of them unannounced, and setting up some checkups soon after others.

But frequent spot checks cost more than big sticks, raising the question of which is more cost effective. A common managerial error is to assume that because frequent audits uncover little behavior that is out of line, less frequent and, therefore, less costly auditing is sufficient. But this assumption overlooks the important deterrent effect of frequent checking. The point is to prevent misconduct, not to catch it.

Rationalization Four:
Because the activity helps the company, the company will condone it and even protect the person who engages in it.

The question to deal with here is "How do we keep company loyalty from going berserk?" At Johns-Manville, a small group of executives and a succession of corporate medical directors kept the facts about the lethal qualities of asbestos from becoming public knowledge for decades, and they managed to live with that knowledge. Johns-Manville, or really the company senior management, did condone their decision and protect those employees. Something similar seems to have happened at General Electric. When one of its missile projects ran a cost greater than the Air Force had agreed to pay, middle managers surreptitiously shifted those costs to projects that were still operating under budget. In this case, the loyalty that ran amok was primarily to the division. Managers want their unit results to look good, but GE, with one of the finest reputations in U. S. industry, was splattered with scandal and paid a fine of 1.4 million dollars. One of the most troubling aspects of the GE case is the company's admission that those involved were thoroughly familiar with the company's ethical standards before the incident took place. This suggests that the practice of declaring a code of ethics and teaching it to employees is not enough to deter unethical conduct. Additional safeguards are needed.

Top management has a responsibility to exert a moral force within the company. Senior executives are responsible for drawing the line between loyalty to the company and action against the laws and values of the society in which the company must operate. Further, because that line can be obscured in the heat of the moment, the line has to be drawn well short of where reasonable men and women could begin to suspect that their rights had been violated. The company has to react long before a prosecutor, for instance, would have a case strong enough to seek an indictment. Executives have a right to expect loyalty from their employees against competitors and detractors, but not loyalty against the law, against common morality, or against society itself. Leaders must warn employees that a disservice to customers, especially to innocent bystanders, cannot be a service to the organization.

Finally, and most important of all, leaders must stress that excuses of company loyalty will not be accepted for acts that place its good name in jeopardy. To put it bluntly, the corporation's leaders must make it clear that employees who harm other people, allegedly for the company's benefit, will be fired. In the end, it is up to top management to send a clear and pragmatic message to all employees that the highest ethical standards will be the foundation of their organization.

Suggested Guidelines for Ethical Decision Making

A fundamental safeguard for making ethical decisions is to ensure that all parties are fully aware of the issues (be sure there is plenty of light on the issue). Whenever in doubt, ask for help. The following process can guide you as you consider ethical decisions. It is important to begin at Step 1 and follow in sequence until you are confident you are making the best decision.

1. Know all the facts.

   - Make sure you have all the facts and information!

2. Is the action legal?

   • If the answer is "No," go no further.

3. Does it comply with company policy?

   • If the answer is "No," there is probably a good reason not to take the action. If you still feel the action is right, ask for advice.

4. Are you (or the other party) expecting something inappropriate or inconsistent with company policy, practice, etc. because of this action?

   • If you are taking this action for material gain, it is probably not ethical.

   • Make sure the action you are taking is to build a relationship with no strings attached and not for personal gain.

5. Who will be impacted by the decision?

   • Will people be positively or negatively impacted by your decision?

6. How will it look if the decision is made public?

   • If you would be ashamed to see a written account of this action in the newspaper, don't do it.

7. Could the action be interpreted as improper?

   • If this action could be perceived as unethical and you may have to explain your actions, either don't do it or ask for advice.

8. Ask.

   • If you get this far and still are concerned or unsure, ask for help.

   • If it's wrong, don't do it.

- If the action clearly breaks company policy and society's values, don't do it.

- If you don't know, ask.

- If you have an ethical issue, ask your manager or other leadership for advice until you get an answer.

Hank Bannister cared about right and wrong. He was proud of his father's business ethic and thought of himself as heir to that ethic. Even so, Hank became a statistic. Arguably, he was a good person who made a bad ethical decision. In the end, Hank asked the question we all ask when we discover the self-inflicted wound: "How could this have happened?"

Sadly, Hank knew all too well the rationalizations which led him to act against the best interest of Bannister Furniture, Bannister's employees, the community, and himself. Hank's failure was the failure to lead himself. Failing to lead himself, he could not lead B.F.L.

6

Leaders Are Empathetic

A leader empathizes with others.
A leader seeks to understand others.

Once upon a time there was a leader named Paul. Paul did not have a university degree. Paul had never been to business school. Paul's exposure to motivational theory was limited to the talks his high school coach used to give Paul and his teammates prior to the big game.

Paul was unorthodox. Even so, he was an effective leader. No one questioned that. People followed Paul instinctively. Given a choice, they chose to follow. Joining Paul's team was a prize employees strove to attain. Paul's motivational strategy brought out the best in people. Peers and associates felt valued and appreciated. Problems were considered normal. Paul viewed problems as nothing more or less than challenges for the team to meet and then to move on. Best of all, as far as the team was concerned, there were no human sacrifices offered up to the god of blame in Paul's department. Everyone shared the credit for success. Everyone was expected to contribute to the analysis and subsequent course correction associated with any failure. But there was no scapegoating.

When outsiders noted Paul's success, they assumed he was a summa cum laude graduate of a major management school. They were surprised to discover he was not. "How, then, could Paul's effectiveness be accounted for?" they frequently asked.

The answer is simple. People followed Paul because he knew first-hand where they were coming from. He knew their dreams, the source of their disappointments, and the hopes they held fragile within themselves. Paul empathized with others. And that was the key to his effectiveness.

Paul believed leadership was all about leading people to believe in themselves. As far as Paul was concerned, there was nothing a leader could not accomplish if who got the credit was not an issue. Paul liked to tell people, with a sparkle of humor in his eye, that he liked to go one step beyond MBWA (Management by Wandering Around). Paul found what he called MBBA (Management by Believing Around) far more effective. He encouraged his people. He took advantage of every opportunity to teach them to believe in themselves. Paul drove confidence, as well as competence, deep into his team. Believing that each person must believe in self before believing in anything else, Paul gave people a sense of confidence. Here's how Paul described his leadership philosophy:

> The longer I live the more I realize the importance of attitude. I suppose that's why I like to tell people, "I've got an attitude and I want you to have one too." Now, wait a minute, don't get me wrong. I'm talking about a **can-do attitude!** A can-do attitude is, to me, more important than the past, than education, than money, than circumstances, than failures, than successes, than what other people think or say. It is more important than appearances, cleverness, or skill. It will make or break a person or a company. The remarkable thing is that we all get to choose our attitude. And, just as remarkable, most of the folks we all work with would like to see each of us get an attitude—a can-do attitude, that is. Oh, I know that some people seem to have built-in filters that screen out boos and amplify hurrahs. But those are the people who never know when they're in trouble. They never let others help them. And people want all the help they can get in succeeding. People just want to know that when the tide comes in all the ships are gonna' be allowed to rise. People want to be able to trust the leader. They want to be able to believe that the leader knows where their vessel is

coming from and how far it has sailed—whether it is a big clipper ship or a small dinghy. They want their effort and their contribution, however small, appreciated. So that brings me back to attitude—in particular, the attitude of the leader. When the leader believes in the team, the team starts to believe in itself. For better or worse, most people live up or down to what is expected of them. The leader gives people a glimpse of what they can be at their best. We cannot change our past. We cannot change the fact that people will act in a certain way. What we can do is play the one hand we have, and that is our attitude. I am convinced that life is ten percent what happens to me and ninety percent how I respond to it. Therefore, a can-do attitude makes all the difference. You want a little pearl of wisdom from me? Well, here it is: Slip another person's shoes off their feet and walk around in their shoes for a while. Then, when you slip them back on the person's feet, make sure they fit better, feel better, and work better. Once you do, that person will follow you and they'll follow, not because they were told to, but because they want to.

Paul knows something profound about the qualities of an effective leader. He knows that the basis of life is people and how they relate to each other. Success, fulfillment, and happiness depend upon our ability to relate effectively. Paul has discovered that the best way to become a person others will follow is to develop the qualities we ourselves are attracted to in others.

If you are attracted to a sense of humor, courage, courtesy, candor, kindness, consideration, competence, good-will, and win-win relationships, then focus on developing these qualities in your own personality. The fact is the qualities we are attracted to in others are the very qualities which attract others to us. People are more alike than they are different. Everyone wants to find both humanity (a sense of compassion) and integrity in a leader.

The key to leading others is empathy. It is putting yourself in the other person's place and, once in the other person's place, demonstrating a sincere desire to know what life and work are like for that person.

How does a leader go about empathizing? Consider for a moment how you want others to treat you. Chances are, the qualities you value are not complicated at all. There's not a person reading this who doesn't like and respond to the following:

- Openness

- Encouragement

- Appreciation

- Forgiveness

- Understanding

First, you want others to be open with you.

You want the people around you to tell you the truth—even when it is unpleasant to hear. This includes not just the obvious that you don't want to be lied to, but also includes the desire that others be candid about what they think and feel. You want to live and work in an environment of openness where there are no hidden agendas. You want others to be open with you, and others want the same quality of openness from you.

Second, you want others to encourage you.

No one ever climbs out of bed in the morning grumbling to himself, "Boy, I hope the boss doesn't encourage me any more today. I don't know how much longer I can handle those 'attaboys.'" People complain, but never about being encouraged to take heart. Few people have more encouragement than they can stand. Think about it; most of your best friends are those who encourage you. You probably don't have many strong relationships with people who put you down. Typically, you avoid such people and seek out those who express belief in you. You want others to encourage you. And others want the same quality of encouragement from you.

Third, you want others to appreciate you.

Motivational theorists have made a convincing case for what they call the deepest principle in human nature—the craving to be appreciated. It is no coincidence that employee satisfaction surveys consistently rank the following as leading causes of employee dissatisfaction:

1. Failure to give credit for suggestions.

2. Failure to respond to grievances.

3. Criticizing employees in front of others.

4. Failure to ask employees their opinions.

5. Failure to provide information, in advance, when changes impact an employee directly.

6. Failure to offer feedback.

7. Failure to encourage.

Notice that every single item has to do with the failure to recognize the importance of the employee. Each item is an affront to the employees' self-esteem and says with clarity, "You don't matter." No one appreciates such treatment. You want others to appreciate you. Others want the same quality of appreciation from you.

Fourth, you want others to forgive you.

If you are like most people, your days include success and failure. The success you can probably handle. The failures, on the other hand, require recovery. Whether it is a failed project or a social gaffe, your course has to be corrected and apologies provided. You recover best when the people involved are willing to grant forgiveness and allow you to move on. You are drawn to people who harbor no grudges and plan no ambushes. You are drawn to people who will grant you another chance to get it right. You want others to forgive you. Others want the same quality of forgiveness from you.

Fifth, you want others to understand you.

How do you feel when you are misunderstood? What kinds of feelings well up inside of you—frustration, disappointment, resentment? These are common responses to being misunderstood.

Peter Drucker, often called the "Father of American Management," claims that sixty percent of all management problems are the result of faulty communications. A leading marriage counselor says that at least half of all divorces are the result of faulty communication between spouses. And, studies have shown that most repeat offenders have difficulty communicating with others. Communication is fundamental to understanding. When someone takes the time to listen to you, you feel they have made an effort to understand you. When someone is open, encouraging, appreciative, and forgiving, you find it easy to believe they are interested in where you are coming from. You want others to understand you. Others want the same quality of understanding from you.

Paul led like the idealized version of the Harvard Business School graduate. However, the secret to Paul's effectiveness lay in his understanding of human nature, not in his education. Paul knew that the basis of life is people and how they relate to each other. Paul gladly walked a mile or more in his employees' shoes. Paul was open with his people. He provided encouragement. He demonstrated appreciation. He forgave their honest mistakes. Paul's empathetic leadership built a high trust, high performance work team.

7

Leaders Communicate

A leader speaks less and listens more.
A leader listens to understand.
A leader speaks to clarify and build trust.

Once upon a time a handyman rang a doorbell in a wealthy neighborhood. Much to his surprise, the handyman was greeted warmly by the lady who came to the door. She stated that she was glad to see him because she had been hoping to find someone to do some painting. "Do you see that bucket of green paint there beside the doorstep?" she asked. "Yes," the man replied. "Well, I've been looking for someone to paint my porch. If you'll just go around back and put a coat of paint on it, I would appreciate it." The man replied, "Thank you," and went to work. A couple of hours later, he rang the doorbell again and informed the lady that the job was complete. She thanked him and said, "Well, let's go look it over." So they went around back and the lady discovered that the man had, in fact, put a nice coat of green paint on her Porsche. When questioned about it, the man explained, "Well, I thought you said to paint your Porsche, I didn't realize you meant porch."

This story illustrates one of the basic principles of communication. It is simply not accurate to assume that when we communicate with others, we transfer a precise piece of information from one mind to another. Words, gestures, and expressions do not, in themselves, have meaning. Instead, people attach meaning to them. Thus, when we attempt to communicate, we always run the risk of engaging in a failure to communicate.

Communication is the exchange of ideas between two people. Effective communication involves more than telling, it involves shared understanding. One-way communication rarely elicits the desired response. It must be understood as a two-way process. In the words of Peter Drucker, "Communications are practically impossible if they are based on a downward relationship." The basic reason for any type of communication is to prompt some form of behavioral response or action. But we often discover that what we say or do does not always elicit the kind of response that we want when we want it. A bank manager asks each of his tellers to ask every customer about opening a new savings account so that the branch can increase the number of new accounts. At the end of the week, there seems to be no increase and furthermore, very few tellers seem to be asking the question. What happened? The president of a software company requests that a proposal for a new client be on her desk the morning of an important meeting. That morning she discovers the proposal is not on her desk and the person responsible is out sick. What happened? These leaders probably did not recognize that successful communication is a two-way street. Although they may have given instructions, they did not really communicate effectively enough to get the desired results.

Before ideas can be accepted, they must be known and understood clearly by the listener. The most valuable contributions to society that we make during our lifetime are often the thoughts and ideas that we communicate. Expressing your creativity is a natural desire that offers a great deal of fulfillment. The more you realize the value of a new idea, the more enthusiastic you become about it. But unless you are able to stimulate the same kind of enthusiasm in others, your idea will begin to gather dust in the closet of your mind. The frustration of your attempt may even stifle future creativity and inhibit your personal growth.

No matter how well informed you may become, no matter how much knowledge you acquire in your chosen field, it is important to remember that very few have ever accomplished much or gone far in any human endeavor without the assistance and cooperation of other people. Friends, relatives, employers, business associates, customers; nearly everyone with whom you are in contact can speed or retard your journey toward your goals. It's easy to see, then, that effective communication and leadership are inseparable. I mentioned earlier that effective communication is a two-way process. However, we often view communication as a way of expressing our ideas to someone else. But we already know that human behavior is not a result of strictly logical and rational thought. Therefore, exchanging facts is only part of the process. The feelings and emotions that develop during the course of conversation strongly influence the behavior of those involved and ultimately the outcome of the conversation. Perhaps an employee enters your office and complains about not having enough time to complete a production report. It would seem that the status of production is being communicated when, in fact, the employee may be saying something very different. The employee may want to communicate the feeling of being overworked or the rationalization of a tendency to procrastinate. The employee may even want you to respond with anger to reinforce his or her own feelings of frustration.

Another example occurs when employees go over the head of their immediate leader in the chain of command. The intent may seem to be to get some action when in reality, perhaps even unknown to the person, the goal is to receive recognition or to undermine the immediate leader's position.

From your vantage point, there are two emotional factors that affect a conversation: 1) How you feel about the other person's ideas and 2) What you believe the other person feels about your ideas. In order for a salesperson to obtain an order, he or she must first discover the prospect's needs, then demonstrate or explain how their product will fill those needs, and finally ask for the order. If the prospect simply says,

"No," but doesn't explain why, the salesperson has no way of overcoming the prospect's objection. The salesperson doesn't know how the prospect really feels and whether or not the objection is actually warranted based on the information presented. Unless the salesperson can find out why the prospect feels the way he or she does, the communication process could come to an abrupt halt.

The same type of communication problem occurs in family relationships. A husband and wife may agree on the fact that they need a new automobile, but the husband discovers that the more he talks about it, the angrier his wife becomes. She certainly agrees outwardly they need a new car, but internally she is thinking about the fact that she will have to cancel the college courses she was planning to take to prepare for a promotion. Until she expresses her feelings, her husband will be unable to understand her actions. Any mention of the car will prompt a heated exchange and will probably affect communication in other areas of their family life.

Once you understand the role that emotions play in communication, you will begin to put yourself in the other person's shoes. As discussed in Chapter VI, this is called *empathy* and is a quality that can be cultivated by developing genuine interest in other people. Don't, however, confuse empathy with nodding your approval, sympathy, or simply agreeing with another person's point of view. Empathy is recognizing the fact that others are entitled to their beliefs just as you are, that they have certain needs to satisfy and goals to achieve just as you do. A doctor who confuses empathy with total agreement could do patients a great disservice. If the doctor agreed with their beliefs about their symptoms, knowing that clinically their appraisal was wrong, his faulty sense of empathy could be fatal. On the other hand, a physician with a good bedside manner is an individual with a strong inherent concern for the patients' needs, anxieties, and problems. The physician uses this emotional understanding to communicate to patients what must be done to affect a cure. As a result, both doctor and patient reach their objectives through mutual understanding. Such understanding may not have been possible without empathy in communication.

To be a truly effective leader, you must develop sensitivity to the needs and wants of your people. The secret is empathy, understanding, and caring. You must communicate through your words and your actions that you are interested in them as individuals. Your employees need to know that you appreciate their efforts and that their accomplishments are recognized. Rewards and recognition need not be expensive. A thank-you note, a pat on the back, or a round of applause can be even more important than monetary rewards.

Knowing your employees' needs, you can chart a course designed to give them what they want and, at the same time, achieve the company's goals. Your own goals may be reached by going around people, through people, or gaining the cooperation of people. It is not difficult to see that the easiest way to accomplish your objectives is with the help of those around you. If you feel that empathy is a characteristic which you need to develop more fully, set some specific goals in the area of personality development. The key to understanding others is to understand yourself. By examining your own experiences, anxieties, and fears, you will be able to relate more closely to the attitudes of others. Remember that your ideas are linked tightly with the results you want to obtain. By keeping your eye on your goals, you will become motivated by results and realize that those goals will only be met through communication that breeds acceptance, understanding, and trust. With this in mind, focus on the needs of others and you will develop empathy in communication.

We communicate every day with different types of people in different types of situations. In order to understand how to get your message across, it is important to examine three fundamental principles of successful, interpersonal communication.

1. The human mind functions in a very orderly fashion. It can only concentrate on one thought at a time. If you attempt to communicate a number of ideas rapidly and in an illogical sequence, the lis-

tener's mind will have great difficulty trying to follow and understand what you are saying. Before you present an idea, make a written plan, highlighting the objectives of your presentation and the main points. Make sure that the important facts are listed in a logical sequence. You may even want to share your presentation with a noninvolved third party to see if he or she clearly understands what is to be presented.

2. The human mind transposes words into pictures. Because words mean different things to different people, the responses that they produce may not be the same for everyone. The level of education, the region of the country that a person comes from, ethnic background—these and many other facts determine what mental pictures crystallize in a person's mind. As you begin to recognize the needs of others, you will use words that elicit an emotional response in harmony with those needs. Such empathy will enhance communications and ensure the accurate perception of your ideas.

3. Too many words clutter up communications. A good example of this was illustrated by an announcement made over a particular company's loud speaker system. It went like this, "Employees of Meniger, Inc. who are desirous of receiving additional copies of the new health benefit form should inform the receptionist of this office of the nature of their request in order to obtain, without delay, the extra copies they should like to have." Think how much simpler this would have been if the announcer had simply said, "If you want additional copies of the new health benefits form, ask the receptionist." When we fail to condense our communication, we leave the door wide open to time consuming misunderstanding and undesired responses. This is especially unfortunate if we need an immediate response to our communication. Become more conscious of your communication style and your ability to empathize with the feelings of others. As you develop a greater sensitivity to the needs and desires of family, friends, and associates, you will

gain their respect and open the door to even more effective communication.

For some reason, many people believe that the ability to speak articulately is an important prerequisite to achievement. Without diminishing the importance of good speech habits, it would serve us well to place greater emphasis on the quality of our listening habits. Benjamin Disraeli noted that nature has given us two ears, but only one mouth. This may be nature's way of telling us that listening is vital to our growth and development. Volumes have been written on the art of public speaking, how to deliver exciting speeches and even how to exercise your vocal chords in order to have a pleasant voice. But little has been written or presented on how to listen for understanding. If we agree that empathy and understanding are important traits, then we realize too that it is impossible to find out what someone else is thinking if we are doing all of the talking. Listening then, becomes our empathy skill.

In order to integrate good listening habits into your personal communication, you must know some of the "how to's" of listening and what to listen for. Here are ten suggestions for developing your listening skills:

1. **Take time to listen.**

    One of the biggest barriers to listening is that most of us have learned not to listen. It is a matter of survival in some sense. With so much racket in the world, we have to select what gets our attention. Tuning out has become such a natural and comfortable habit, we sometimes forget to tune in again, even when we need to. Listening is work, but it's worth the effort. So when you enter a situation where you know you need to listen, discipline yourself to enter a tuned-in mode. Bear down, suppress other thoughts, and focus. In time, the discipline of listening will become second nature, but only if it is practiced.

2. **Be attentive**.

Another natural inclination for listeners is to race ahead of the speaker—to jump to conclusions, prepare a response, or mentally criticize what the speaker is saying. The solution is to respond to the speaker every step of the way. Maintain eye contact. If you find your eyes drawn away, your mind won't be far behind. Also, demonstrate your interest by nodding, saying "uh-huh," and adopting an alert leaned-in posture. This will let the speaker know you care. He or she is far more likely to tell you what you need to know, and you are more likely to hear it. People talk about what is important to them. Whether you agree on the importance of the statement or issue, your lack of attention will be perceived as a lack of respect for their thoughts and opinions. Attentive listening, at its very best, means caring enough to take the time to pay attention. Easy to say—tough to do. Hearing involves focusing, being attentive to the individual and what is being said.

3. **Do not talk when you are listening**.

It is like talking with your mouth full—it's rude. It is easy for a conversation to degenerate into nothing more than alternating monologues. There is a difference in listening and waiting for your turn to talk. At the very least, constantly interrupting the speaker communicates insensitivity. At the worst, it is a subtle power play that leaves the other person feeling discounted and ignored.

4. **Listen with an open mind**.

Most of us have a natural tendency to hear what we want to hear. On the other hand, we also tend to filter out what we do not want to hear. For example, suppose a colleague tells you, "I'll have that project ready for you on Wednesday if all the materials come in." Because you want the project completed by Wednesday, you latch on to the first part of the statement. You make your plans with the expectation that Wednesday is the day. It is not until Wednesday and the project isn't done because the materials didn't come in, that you remember everything that was said. It's important to listen with an open mind. When you open your mind and approach a topic from the other person's point of view, you have a good chance to round out a complete picture of the facts surrounding the situation. Once you prove yourself capable of doing this, the other person is inclined to want to prove that he or she is just as capable of being fair and open minded as you are.

5. **Listen to more than the words**.

Research indicates that at least sixty percent of a speaker's message is communicated nonverbally through tone of voice, facial expressions, and body language. Much of this information is received and processed unconsciously. Although you're unaware of it, your brain makes hundreds of calculations per second. When you're listening to someone, consider his or her posture, intonation, facial expressions, and gestures. Be careful not to give these non-verbals more weight than they deserve; however, trust your intuition. If a message sounds right, yet feels wrong, a red flag has been raised. Look and listen a little closer, and you will be glad you did. Listen for feelings. People tend to repeat those things that are important to them. Listen not only to what they say, but how they say it. Voices express emotion through pitch, intonation, hesitation, and speed of delivery. By listening to what people say and how they say it, you will discover the feelings behind the words.

6. **Ask questions politely**.

One of the best techniques for attentive listening is asking questions. This can be particularly effective with people who ramble—it helps them focus, it lets them know you are serious about gaining needed information. If you are dealing with a rambler, feel free to interrupt occasionally, politely of course, with a question. It encourages them to come to the point. Questioning also works well with shy or inarticulate people. Letting them know exactly what you're looking for makes the conversation easier for them.

7. **Don't shoot the messenger.**

Sometimes people, particularly busy, task oriented people, fly off the handle when they hear bad news. Have you ever been guilty of this reaction? If you want people to cover up problems and keep the hard facts from coming to the surface, this approach works well. If, on the other hand, you want to be kept abreast of the information you need to do your job, stay calm. Welcome the arrival of bad news. In many instances, it is more valuable than good news. Let the people around you know that you want the facts whether the facts are good or bad.

8. **Take selective notes.**

It can be difficult to listen and write at the same time; however, it is essential in business to have an accurate recall of what was said. The pitfall is that you may be too busy writing to keep up with what is being said. The trick is to take selective notes, writing down key words, phrases, concepts and statistics. Try not to be too conspicuous. The speaker could be intimidated if you take down every word he or she says. And, in the event you are having a one-to-one conversation, you may want to say to the other person, "I need to keep a record of what we're saying. My memory is not great, so please don't be offended. I'm just trying to keep up with the important points we have agreed to."

9. **Get to "yes" or "no."**

Sometimes you need a quick answer without all the details. Under time constraints, consider saying, "I need a yes or no answer." Or, "Please briefly give me your best insight at this moment." "Give me a headline," can also work. People are accustomed to newspaper headlines delivering the essence of the story. Most of all, when you need a brief, to the point answer, ask for the person's help in getting the information as quickly as possible. This appeals to the better nature of most people. Not all, but most of us like to think of ourselves as helpful. However, rushing to the core of the issue must not be the pattern of your communication, it must be only an occasional event.

10. **Summarize**.

This is absolutely essential in those situations where you have to understand exactly what is said. When the speaker comes to a natural pause after finishing a point, paraphrase what he or she has said. Begin the summary with a phrase such as, "This is what I heard you say." Or, "My understanding of what you said is..." Then ask the speaker if what you heard or understood is correct. This provides the speaker with an opportunity to clarify or confirm what he or she said.

You can use these helpful hints regularly in your communication efforts. As others notice your attentiveness to their remarks, they will no doubt increase their respect for you and your concern for their feelings. People want you to believe in them just as you want them to believe in you. When you display empathy for another human being, you heighten self respect. The most loved, the most respected, and most successful leaders everywhere are invariably those who have the capacity to empathize with the feelings of others and who openly show it. Good listeners are good empathizers. In fact, the best way to express your interest and your empathy for another is to simply listen.

8

Leaders Are Mentors

A leader is honest, rational and civil.
A leader values common sense.
A leader honors basic human dignity.

Once upon a time there was a woman named June. June was the widow of a successful entrepreneur. Over a period of twenty-six years her late husband, Walter, had built a family-owned corner drugstore into a chain of 58 stores with annual sales in excess of one hundred, eighty-six million dollars.

June and Walter were the parents of one son, Michael. Michael was a high school sophomore when his father died. Therefore, his entry into the family business had to wait. As Michael grew toward adulthood and completed college, his mother assumed (though she never actually discussed it with him) that Michael would follow in his father's footsteps. Michael would someday run Double Discount Drugs. As president and CEO, Michael would fulfill his father's dream of one hundred stores with annual sales of over two hundred million. This, June believed, was the only course her son's life could take.

June was to be disappointed. When Michael completed undergraduate school, he announced he would not be entering the family business. Greatly distraught, June went to see an old family friend and confidante. In a matter of minutes she poured out her disappointment. The old friend, who happened to be a retired high school principal, listened patiently as June wandered through various stages of grief—denial, anger, depression and back to anger. June's pain was not new to the former principal. He had witnessed this frustration in other parents. He knew June's disappointment was genuine, so he agreed to have a talk with Michael.

Michael arrived for their appointment early. Rather than being reluctant to talk, Michael jumped right into the reasons for his decision. Michael explained, "I would have loved to take over the family business. But you need to understand the relationship I had with my father. He was a driven man who came up the hard way. His objective was to teach me self-reliance, but he made a mistake by trying to teach me that principle in a way that was demoralizing. He thought the best way to teach me self-reliance was to never encourage or praise me. He wanted me to be tough and independent."

"Two or three times every week we played catch in the yard. Sometimes we'd play catch with a baseball, at other times with a football. Either way the goal was always the same. I was to catch the ball ten times straight. I would catch that ball eight or nine times, but always on the tenth throw, he would do anything to make me miss. He would throw it on the ground or over my head, but always so I had no chance of catching it."

Michael paused for a long moment and then finished, "He never let me catch the tenth ball—never! No matter how hard I tried, he always set me up to fail. And I guess that's why I have to get away from my father's business; I want to catch the tenth ball."

Michael's father believed character and leadership are developed through the arbitrary exercise of authority. Nothing could be further from the truth. Both character and leadership are developed through the power of personal influence. Walter believed he was preparing Michael to be president of Double Discount Drugs. He failed to recognize the top three responsibilities of a mentor: to nurture, to encourage, and to set the person up to succeed.

Leadership is an art. Therefore, it cannot be taught as a science (i.e., catch a set number of balls and you qualify). Leadership is not the hammering out of an authoritarian skilled in the arbitrary exercise of power. Leadership is the weaving of a relationship. That relationship, woven well, results in mutual trust and influence. At its core, effective leadership is the capacity to influence the behavior of another due to the quality of the relationship.

Personal influence is, more than anything else, an ethical dynamic. The myth is that leaders transmit the values of the organization. The truth is that leaders are the values of the organization. Leaders do not merely relay a message to employees; leaders are the message. This is why the best evidence of effective leadership is found primarily in the followers. Thus, leaders have a moral obligation to be honest, rational, and civil in relating to followers and all other persons. Leaders have a moral obligation to set people up to succeed.

For example, have you ever observed two managers of equal position, rank, and authority within an organization? One leader's objectives seem to be successfully accomplished with a degree of ease. The other leader seems to always be under the gun, resolving one crisis after another by throwing around authority. If you have witnessed this dynamic, then you know firsthand that persons of equal authority do not necessarily possess the same degree of power. What is the difference between authority and personal power? The concepts have been used interchangeably over the years. However, they are not the same.

Personal power is the capacity to act in ways which influence the behavior of others. It is a personal attribute, and like all personal attributes, it can be developed. It is a skill leaders develop in their everyday relationships with reports, peers, superiors, and friends. Personal power is granted to the leader by those who trust and believe in the character of the leader. The leader *earns* personal power. It is not a part of the authority the organization bestows along with a title. It is won in the trenches of the workday. It is won through honest, rational, and civil treatment of others.

Authority, on the other hand, may be defined as a contractual right granted by an organization in keeping with a position. It is a right granted by the organization to organize work, settle disputes, control operations, make and implement decisions, administer, and manage. It is, in a nutshell, the right to be the boss.

A leader who abuses authority diminishes his or her personal power and, ultimately, the ability to influence others. People subjected to constant use or abuse of authority will develop subtle and effective ways of subverting it in order to protect themselves. Excessive use of authority often produces behavior in others which resembles the reaction of a child responding to restrictions imposed by a parent. The child rebels, not necessarily because the parent's expectations are unreasonable, rather because they are imposed through the exercise of authority—"Do it because I said so. I'm the parent and you're not." Typically, authority diminishes rather than enhances an adult-to-adult relationship in the work environment.

Authority does fill a necessary and important function in the life of an organization and can be an efficient tool of management when used judiciously. An effective leader will not shun the use of authority when the situation demands it but will avoid creating situations in which authority is the only recourse.

Authority has no chance of assuming its appropriate place in an organization (much less a relationship) if it is exercised arbitrarily or as a means of manipulating others. In that context, Michael is not the exception. Michael is the rule. People will simply not accept being set up to fail again and again; they instinctively know such an arrangement is unfair. The relationship between a leader and a follower has ethical implications. Among those implications are the follower's right to be treated fairly and the leader's obligation to qualify for the right to lead by being open, honest, and fair.

More than likely, Michael's father was well-intentioned. He very much wanted to nurture in his son those qualities essential to effective leadership. Unfortunately, he forgot that relationships count more than structure. There was something Michael needed prior to the ability to run Double Discount Drugs. Michael needed to believe his father wanted a relationship with him. He needed to believe his father would invest in his success. Michael wanted from his father what every follower wants from every leader—a reason to believe the relationship matters. This means relating to others in a fundamentally responsible manner. It means going far beyond the expediency of treating others as little more than a means to an end. It means asking the ethical question: What is the right thing to do?

The right thing to do may depend, to some extent, on the situation and context. However, whatever the situation or context, certain ethical mandates always apply. The leader has a moral obligation to be honest, rational, and civil in relating to others. This is not slightly less true as it applies to a subordinate. If anything, it is all the more essential in relationships with subordinates. The measure of a leader's character is not how he or she relates to a peer or superior. The measure of a leader's character is the degree to which he or she is honest, rational, and civil in relating to a follower (subordinate). This is why principled leaders are the last boy and girl scouts in a society increasingly in need of honest, rational, and civil leadership. And, not by coincidence, this often determines how successful a leader will be in developing personal power. Honest, rational, and civil behavior are foundational to building personal power.

First, honesty is the cornerstone of ethical leadership. It means truth-telling to be sure. It includes a commitment to being candid. However, in this context, it can best be described by the word quality. Typically, we use the word quality to describe products, services, or both. It is also a good word to use in talking about the quality of our relationships, and the quality of our communications, and the quality of our promises to each other. Also, it is reasonable to think about quality in terms of truth and integrity.

If you look up integrity in the dictionary, you will discover that, among other definitions, integrity is: A) *The quality of a relationship;* and B) A cross-reference to the word honor. There you will discover that honor means a *fine sense of one's obligations.* Clearly quality, integrity, and honor are the supporting pillars of honesty. The result is what Abraham Lincoln called "the honorable obligations of honesty."

The question follows: What are the honorable obligations of honesty? The answer can be best understood in the context of rights, obligations, and responsibilities. Followers have certain rights. Leaders have certain obligations. Leaders and followers are bound by mutual responsibilities. These mutual responsibilities include the following rights and obligations:

The right to understand. Everyone has a right to understand his or her environment. This includes the right to be provided with information about decisions, events, or issues which impact us directly. Leaders have an obligation to create opportunities for understanding, whether through meetings, newsletters, or one-to-one conversations. Leaders and followers are bound by a mutual commitment to use all information (whether it is information concerning persons or the organization) responsibly.

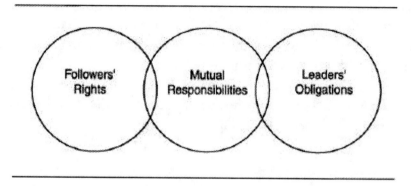

The right to contribute. Everyone has a right to be needed by the organization. This is the right to contribute to organizational success and to share the reward and satisfaction of achievement. Leaders have an obligation to ensure employees have clearly defined and measurable goals and to recognize employees for their contributions. Leaders and followers are mutually responsible for setting each other up to make a valued contribution.

The right to ownership. Everyone has a right to be involved in the decision-making process at some level. This provides a sense of ownership—the sense that my life and work is, to some degree, within my control. A sense of ownership also bolsters self-esteem. Leaders have an obligation to solicit input from team members and assure that the way work gets done does not demean the people involved. Leaders and followers are equally responsible for following through on their ownership commitments.

The right to be accountable. Everyone has a right to know how they are doing. Without feedback on performance it may be difficult, even impossible, for a person to grow, develop, and meet personal and organizational needs. Every team member has a right to know when his or her performance is unacceptable. Leaders have an obligation to provide team members with candid, constructive feedback. To withhold feedback is to deny the team member the opportunity to improve. Followers have a responsibility to consider constructive feedback in a context of goodwill.

The right to appeal. Everyone has a right to appeal or challenge the decision of a leader without the threat of retribution. This ensures that authority will not be used arbitrarily. Typically, the knowledge that I can appeal is as important as the appeal itself. Leaders have an obligation to provide open, non-threatening access to the appeal process. Leaders and followers are mutually responsible for:

- talking to each other, not about each other.

- owning what I say: I must be willing to say in your presence anything I would say in your absence.

- ensuring each person's freedom to talk with any person in the organization, regardless of department or title.

- closing the loop. I may go over my boss' head, but he or she must be brought into the loop prior to final resolution.

Second, the ethical leader has an obligation to be rational. Rational leadership is defined primarily by a leader's decision (and it is a decision) to be guided by reasonable expectations. The **rational** leader is a **reasonable** person.

The reasonable leader is a leader who brings a good measure of common sense to all issues. This means, among other things, that a rational leader will not require team members to be super-human—working long hours for an indefinite period of time, isolated from family, friends, and normal, healthy, life-enriching opportunities. Such common sense understands the reasonable constraints of doing business.

The leader has an obligation to assure the success of the organization. However, such effort must be tempered by a bottom-line ethical reality. Every legitimate organization has a right to survive, but it does not have the right to survive at any cost. Resisting the temptation to survive at any cost includes obeying the law, providing a safe work environment, and ensuring equitable pay. Just as essential as responsible leadership is the obligation to relate to team members in an ethically rational manner. Rational leadership includes the following obligations:

1. **Assuring informed consent.**

   People should be provided enough information to enable them to make an informed decision. Looking for a reason not to withhold information should be the norm. Withholding information should be the exception. Requiring a person to make a decision with inadequate information, particularly if the information is being deliberately withheld, is unreasonable and unethical.

2. **Eliminating bogus time constraints.**

   Manipulating a person through bogus time constraints holds the potential of setting the person up to fail. Sometimes decisions have to be made and actions have to be taken in very tight time frames; however, this is not always the case. Rational leadership carries the responsibility of the long view. Not just the long view in strategic terms, but in people terms. Looking ahead and anticipating what decisions will need to be made is an essential element of effective leadership. This includes providing team members with as much time as possible to think and decide.

3. **Respecting the conscience of others.**

   No two persons experience reality exactly the same way. It is rare for two people to have in common an identical set of life experiences. Such diversity is normal, but can result in disagreements on the basis of conscience. The rational leader wants people to succeed or fail on the basis of performance, not on the basis of religion, political affiliation, or life-style choice. The only way to avoid conflicts of conscience is to respect the conscience of others.

Third, civility is vital to the success of any organization. Though often underrated and neglected, civility oils the machinery of human interaction. Successful organizations are built on cooperation. Effective leaders know the critical role civility plays in sustaining cooperation. Respect for others and consideration for their feelings are the attributes of a courteous person. Everyone, without exception, appreciates being treated with courtesy. It is the most up-front means we have of knowing that we are valued. Disrespect expressed through attitude, action, or conversation sends a clear message: *You are of lesser value than I.* Such an idea is unacceptable. Simple courtesy is the minimum civility due employees. When our mothers' taught us to use the magic words, *please* and *thank you*, they were right on target. Courtesy costs nothing. It may, however, generate an unlimited return.

A great deal of money is spent each year educating employees on the importance of courtesy when dealing with customers and business associates. But an organization does not become imbued with courtesy just by talking it up. One cannot buy courtesy, nor does it come as a result of an official request. All efforts to develop good manners among employees are a waste of time unless the leadership is as courteous toward employees as it would have them be toward peers and customers.

The practice of courtesy within an organization must begin with the leadership. It must extend from the top to the bottom. It must include everyone, particularly those who have no authority or position which might be thought of as commanding respect. Simply stated, it means that the same simple, human courtesy granted to the president of the organization must be granted to the secretary, the frontline supervisor, or the custodian.

The good manners of the leadership have a profound effect on the cooperation and effort put forward throughout the organization. A leader who is courteous to reports inspires civility, and the cumulative result is a department where there is teamwork and minimum friction.

The myth is that civility is indicative of weakness. Nothing could be further from the truth. Courtesy is not a sign of weakness; it denotes the self-confidence and inner strength so necessary to self-discipline. People respect the leader who treats others with courtesy, attracting the best people and the best *from* people. People who possess dignity and self-respect want to work with a leader whose attitude toward them is friendly and courteous, the minimum requirement for a successful relationship.

Here are some behaviors to keep in mind as you lead your team to greater civility.

- Treat everyone with the same courtesy you would extend to the president of the company.

- Use (but don't overuse) the magic words *please* and *thank you*.

- Avoid petty or mean-spirited comments about others.

- Make sure your humor is not at the expense of another.

- Be open to being *wrong*.

- When proven wrong, be quick to acknowledge that you were wrong.

- When appropriate, be quick to offer an apology.

- Speak to people.

- Call people by name.

- When people come to your office, treat them as guests in your home—offer them something to drink.

- When you visit the office of a report, act as if you were a guest in another person's home.

- Don't second guess the motives of others.

- Don't patronize.

- Tell the truth with compassion.

A quick survey of human behavior will demonstrate that few things are as uncommon as common sense. Arguably, this observation falls in the same category as "the obvious is not always obvious." For example, to one on the outside looking in, it would seem obvious common sense that Michael would want to catch the tenth ball. That bit of common sense was lost of his father, Walter.

It may be obvious that leaders must be honest, rational, and civil, but every employee can relate at least one story that proves common sense does not come with a job title. Leaders who would be mentors must first lead themselves through honest, rational, and civil behavior—then and only then, can a leader nurture (mentor) those qualities in others.

9

Leaders Motivate

A leader leads others to lead themselves.

Once upon a time a wealthy entrepreneur bought a huge ranch in Wyoming. As soon as he was settled, he invited some of his closest associates to see it. After touring some of the 3,500 acres of mountains and rivers and grasslands, he ushered everybody into the house. The house was as spectacular as the scenery, and out back was the largest swimming pool anyone had ever seen. However, it was not a pool in which anyone would want to swim. The pool was filled with alligators and poisonous snakes of every description.

The eccentric owner explained, "I value courageous risk-taking above everything else. As far as I'm concerned, the courage to take a risk is what made me a billionaire. In fact, I think that courage is such a powerful virtue I'll make each of you the same offer. The first person who is courageous enough to dive in that pool and swim the length of it can have his choice of my house, my land, or my money." Of course everybody had a good laugh at the rancher's robust, but absurd, challenge and proceeded to follow the owner into the house for lunch.

Suddenly, the clamor of footsteps and laughter was interrupted by a splash! Turning around, they saw one of their number swimming for his life across the pool, thrashing at the water as the snakes and alligators swarmed after him. After several death-defying seconds, the man climbed out of the pool, unharmed, on the other side.

The host was absolutely amazed, but stuck to his promise. He said, "You are indeed a man of courage, and I will stand by my word. What do you want? You can have your choice—my house, my land, my money—just name it and it's yours." The young man looked at him with anger and revenge in his eyes and said, "Mr., all I want is the name of the guy who pushed me into the pool."

There are many misconceptions about motivation. One of the most common is the belief that motivation is nothing more than a sophisticated form of manipulation. The effective practitioner, this theory holds, would not have to push anyone in the pool or call out the snakes and alligators. The effective manipulator simply offers the appropriate carrot. The carrot, presented with the right measure of enthusiasm, will do the job. Men and women will jump in the pool in droves. This is the most common motivational myth.

Persuading a person to do something for your reasons and not for their reasons is not motivation. It is manipulation. Nor is motivation pushing someone to take what they otherwise believe is the wrong course of action. That is intimidation. Both manipulation and intimidation will often move a person to action. They will not, however, motivate a person.

That brings us to the second most common misconception about motivation: Once you have persuaded a person to move, you have effectively motivated him. Leaders frequently ask and seek to answer the question which follows this assumption: What is the simplest, surest, and most direct way of getting someone to do something? The answer, of course, is to ask. And, if the person does not want to do it? Demand that it be done! This is the last and first resort of the dictatorial leader who may add, without blushing, "Punish those who disobey." This type of leader will get results. The surest way of getting someone to do something with the greatest economy of words is to make sure there is a heavy price for not doing what is asked. But this is not motivation. It is just another form of manipulation called intimidation.

Manipulation masquerading as motivation comes in many forms. Here are just a few:

Physical Intimidation/Threat

This is a literal application of the concept and was frequently used in the past. It has, however, four major drawbacks: 1) It diminishes any sense of good will the employee might have toward the organization; 2) It is inconsistent with the image of benevolence most organizations cherish; 3) Since it is a physical attack, the employee may feel compelled to kick back; 4) Physical intimidation/threat does not work.

Negative Psychological Intimidation

Negative psychological intimidation seeks to motivate by manipulating a person's emotional vulnerabilities. Under this theory, ego sores are rubbed raw by snubbing, ignoring, discounting a person's contributions, by-passing, reducing compensation, relocating to a smaller office, taking away perks without explanation, and countless other methods of supposedly motivating another through emotional intimidation.

Negative psychological intimidation has several advantages over physical intimidation. First, the cruelty is not visible; the bleeding is internal and comes much later. Second, the victim will not kick back since he has not actually been kicked. Third, since the number of psychological pains that a person can feel is unlimited, the impact may linger for hours or days. Fourth, the person administering the kick can appear to be perfectly innocent of any wrongdoing. Fifth, those who practice it receive some ego satisfaction (one-up-manship). Finally, the employee who does complain can always be accused of being paranoid since there is no tangible evidence of an actual attack. However, negative psychological intimidation does have one thing in common with physical intimidation—it does not work. It does demonstrate how unscrupulous an unprincipled leader can be.

What does negative psychological intimidation accomplish? If a person is subjected to physical or psychological intimidation, who is motivated? The intimidator is motivated, the intimidated is not. Intimidation does not lead to motivation. It leads to movement. Alligators and snakes will get movement out of any sane individual. However, alligators and snakes will produce movement only as long as they are present. Even this is unreliable because some people tame the alligators and snakes. So you're left trying to find another way to frighten/intimidate employees into movement.

Positive Manipulation

Most leaders are quick to see that psychological or physical intimidation is not motivation. On the other hand, many continue to believe that positive manipulation is motivation. If the leader says to the employee, "Do this for the company, and in return I will give you a reward, an incentive, more status, a promotion, all the quid pro quos that exist in an organization," is this motivation? Many leaders would answer with a resounding "yes." The reality, however, is far different.

I have a Border Collie named Princess. Let's say that when Princess was a puppy and I wanted her to move, I kicked her in the rear and she moved. Now that I have finished her obedience training, I hold up a dog biscuit whenever I want her to move. In this example, who is motivated—me or the dog? Princess wants the biscuit, but I want Princess to move. I am the one who is motivated, and Princess is the one who moves. All I did was apply manipulation frontally; I exerted a pull instead of a push. When an organization wishes to use a positive manipulation, it has available a variety of dog biscuits to wave in front of the employee to get him to jump (move).

Perhaps, you are thinking, negative intimidation is a no-brainer. It is disruptive to the individual and the organization, and it moves people but does not motivate them. What is so bad about dangling a carrot in front of an employee? Positive manipulation gets people moving with no hard feelings whatsoever.

Intimidation is easily recognized and rejected because it is raw force. Positive manipulation seems harmless because it is seduction. However, in this context, it is worse to be seduced than to be intimidated. Intimidation is a sinister act carried out by a deviant. Both the victim and the culprit are easily identified. Seduction, on the other hand, means you were party to your own manipulation. The organization does not have to kick you; you kick yourself.

Alligators and Carrots versus Entrepreneurs

Manipulation, whether negative or positive, is not motivation. It is movement and only movement. If I kick my dog from the front or the rear, she will move. And when I want her to move again, I have to kick her again. In the same way, I can charge a person's battery, and then recharge it, and recharge it again. But it is only when the person has his own generator that he is motivated. The person then needs no outside stimulation. He *wants* to do it. Alligators and carrots generate movement. Ownership and pride of workmanship generate motivation. It is the team member as entrepreneur that creates motivation. The team member must have a compelling reason to ask and act on a single question: What would I do if this business were mine? How then, do leaders give team members a compelling reason to ask and answer that question? How do leaders create a sense of ownership? How do leaders make entrepreneurs (a company of one) out of the people on the line?

The motivational theorist Frederick Herzberg gives us a framework for answering these questions. First, what are often thought of as motivators are actually only satisfiers. A satisfier is anything in the work environment which assures a level playing field. It is any aspect of work which, when met, becomes a neutral issue in the work environment. It satisfies, but does not motivate. This is not to say that satisfiers are unimportant. They are very important inasmuch as they create an environment which management and employees find mutually beneficial.

Satisfiers include:

- Company policy & procedure

- Employee relationship with leaders

- Work conditions (safety, cleanliness, et cetera)

- Compensation

- Relationship with peers

- Status

- Security

- Participation in decision making

Much of the positive manipulation developed in an attempt to create motivation is not a motivator at all—it is a satisfier.

These bogus motivators (which are in fact, satisfiers) include:

- **Reducing time spent at work.** This is done in the belief that additional time away from work will motivate a person when at work. The fact is that while motivated people do not necessarily work longer hours, they do not watch the clock either.

- **Increased wages.** This satisfier only motivates people to seek the next increase. It rarely motivates a person to be a self-starter or to work smarter. Good pay is a satisfier and an important one.

- **Benefits.** This became a satisfier in the U. S. Corporate Culture more than forty years ago. Employees believe vacations, health insurance, retirement, etc. are an entitlement due them as members of the organization.

- **The Big Picture.** The belief that employees only need to see where they fit in the big picture to be motivated is bogus. A guy tightening a thousand bolts a day just needs to know he is building a Buick, and he will be motivated. While most employees welcome information about the organization, once again, they consider it their right to know such information. Therefore, information is a satisfier.

- **Sensitivity Training.** If leaders and employees only understood themselves better as individuals by going through individual or group therapy, they would be motivated. While any effort to enhance self-understanding and human relations skills is commendable (even necessary in some instances), sensitivity training is, at best, a satisfier. It is not a motivator.

In contrast to satisfiers, motivators engage the *magic of the human heart*. Motivators awaken the internal generator which enables employees to charge their own battery. Motivators create owners. Owners are entrepreneurs. An entrepreneur is a company of one. What then, are motivators? Motivators are few in number but critical in mass. One well-engaged motivator will impact performance more than a dozen of the most creative satisfiers.

Motivators include:

- **Achievement:** The personal satisfaction which comes from having set a goal and paid the price to reach it. A word of caution: This only works if the employee is a part of the goal-setting process.

- **Pride in Workmanship:** The enhanced self-esteem which comes from having done a job as well or better than anyone else (world class quality).

- **Ownership:** The responsibility for oneself and one's work. This includes the opportunity to try, to fail, to learn, and to move on—to be trusted to take responsible risks.

- **Growth:** The opportunity to become more than I am; the opportunity for greater achievement, responsibility, and recognition. Growth is knowledge that I can increase my value to myself and to the organization.

- **Recognition:** The affirmation of my value and contribution, to be appreciated, thanked, and respected for the contribution I have made. This includes, of course, the opportunity to benefit from my contribution.

You have probably noticed that in describing motivators we have also described the entrepreneurial spirit at its best! Achievement, pride of workmanship, and ownership drive and motivate the Team Member as Entrepreneur to ask and answer the big question: What would I do if this business were mine? The Motivation Continuum on page 92 illustrates how leaders create The Team Member as Entrepreneur.

Entrepreneurial team members will view themselves as a company of one. They will see the work to be done as "my work." They will accept responsibility for themselves and their work. The myth that only a few people in the organization are capable of self-management will have to be put aside. In order for the job itself to change, the content of the job must change. It is the content of the job which will create motivation. Attitudes about being involved or challenged, are important, but not as important as the content. The organization will have to trust itself to the competence of the entrepreneur as team member. Fundamentally, this is achieved through employee-centered leadership, as illustrated on page 92. The degree to which the employee is granted freedom/responsibility (horizontal scale) is the degree to which the employee will accept ownership (left vertical scale). In contrast, the degree to which the leader exercises control is the degree to which the employee abdicates responsibility/ownership and is demotivated.

The following principles demonstrate employee-centered leadership which creates ownership in an organization.

Employee-Centered Leadership Principle	*Motivators Involved*
1. Removing some controls while retaining accountability	Ownership and personal achievement
2. Increasing employee's accountability for his or her own work	Responsibility, recognition, and pride in workmanship
3. Giving a person a complete natural unit of work (module, division, area, etc.)	Ownership, achievement, pride in workmanship, and recognition
4. Granting additional authority in his or her budget	Ownership, achievement, and recognition.
5. Making periodic reports directly available to the employee.	Growth, recognition and pride in workmanship.
6. Introducing new and more difficult tasks not previously handled	Growth and recognition.
7. Assigning individuals specific or specialized tasks, enabling them to become experts.	Ownership, growth, pride in workmanship, and recognition.
8. Encourage and facilitate the employees' continuing education.	Achievement, growth and recognition.

The Motivation Continuum

Boss-centered leadership

Employee-centered leadership

Exercise of Authority / Control of Manager

Area of Employee Freedom / Responsibility

10 9 8 7 6 5 4 3 2 1

Leader makes decision and announces it.

Leader "sells" decision.

Leader presents ideas and invites questions.

Leader presents tentative decision subject to change.

Leader presents problem, gets suggestions, makes decision.

Leader defines limits asks group to make decision.

Leader permits employee to function within limits defined by team/ leadership.

Finally, the argument for employee-centered leadership can be summed up as follows: The most effective way to motivate an employee is to grant the employee ownership of, and accountability for, meaningful work from which he can realize pride of workmanship. Employees can be pushed or pulled into movement by an alligator or carrot. However, people do their best for their own reasons. And people do their best for their own reasons because every person has a fundamental need to matter.

For most people, pride of workmanship and the opportunity to do meaningful work are expressions of their need to matter. Employees work for what their efforts will bring to themselves and to the people they love and care about. The leader who would lead others to lead themselves understands that work is not just work. A job well done and valued by the organization helps define the degree to which an employee will realize his or her need to be challenged, appreciated, and praised. Everyone has a heart they would gladly give to a place where they know they matter. This is motivation. This is the magic of the human heart.

10

Leaders Provide Performance Management

A leader is candid.
A leader tells the truth with compassion.

Once upon a time there was a vice president of engineering named Leo. Leo's company made fine-quality capital goods equipment. He had been with the company for thirty-five years. Leo was a good engineer who knew the product inside and out, and through the years he had come to know the customers as well. He felt proud of and personally involved in the installation of the product. It was not unusual to see him coatless and with his tie loose, perched on a stool before a drafting board surrounded by young engineers, digging at a tough installation problem. While some thought Leo did too much himself, others felt that with him on the job the customer would be satisfied.

One day, however, the company became a wholly owned subsidiary when the president, whose family owned the company, sold it to a large corporation. One allied product line was acquired, then another. Finally, Leo's department was asked to do the engineering work for several subsidiaries not set up to do their own.

Now Leo's job had changed, subtly but surely, and trouble began to brew for Leo because he couldn't seem to change with the situation.

Psychologically, Leo saw himself as a one man department (with assistants as trainees) who personally engineered the product for the customer, his friend. He resisted the impersonality of working on the engineering problems of sister companies whose customers and products he barely knew and cared less about. The new-fangled system of a home office staff engineering vice president seemed just another unnecessary complication. Nothing worked the way it used to. Leo saw himself bypassed by progress and change, and he did not like it.

So, unconsciously, Leo began to resist and to fight. His yearning for the good ole days forced him into a fast run to know more customers and more product lines, to work more evenings, and to press new systems into the form of old procedures. And, of course, he began to slip. Gradually, Leo came to be viewed by his superiors as good ole Leo. The idea now voiced by his superiors was, "Let's not let Leo in on this matter or he'll take it over himself and we'll get bogged down!" His direct reports considered Leo a fine fellow but a bit old-fashioned.

Fortunately, before the situation forced a major organizational shift, Leo took stock of his situation and really saw himself as he was. His self-image of a personal engineer was no longer applicable to the corporation's greatly expanded needs. And right then with this new glimpse of himself and the courage and self-honesty to face it, he began to change. He started by focusing on how his years of experience could be applied to the coaching of his direct reports. He consciously placed himself in the shoes of staff vice president of engineering. He began to understand how to better mesh gears with the new reality of the world around him. He stopped resisting the newfangled data processing and automation procedures. Leo began the most challenging re-engineering job of his career—changing Leo. In the process, Leo gained a powerful professional insight: The more realistic one's view of self, the greater the degree of personal effectiveness.

As Leo thought through this discovery, he realized that what he needed to do with Leo was what he had always done with equipment and processes: Be doggedly committed to the truth. Leo needed to apply to his self-concept the same capacity to critique which he routinely applied to his work. Leo realized that his image of himself functioned like a filter. Without self-critique, self-concept screens out what each person does not want to hear and see, and allows through only the information the person wants to see and hear. Utilizing his excellent problem-solving skills, Leo accurately concluded that you cannot (will not) fix what is broken until you admit that it is broken. Nothing changes until it becomes what it is.

However, this was only the beginning of Leo's new insight. With his greater capacity to self-critique, Leo acquired greater control over the thing he wants most to have control over: his destiny. Through self-critique, Leo could take charge of his own development and, therefore, take charge of his future. Even more exciting was Leo's recognition that the capacity to self-critique had important implications for his team, a concept he was learning to understand and use. Self-critique can lay the groundwork for insight, without which growth or change will not occur. Feedback (critique) from superiors, peers, and team members can provide the same level of growth and development born of shared insight.

Admitting that he could not do everything was tough for Leo. Accepting the fact that he was not right was even tougher. How does one gain such insight? How do individuals discover that not only can they change but they should change? Unfortunately, for those who like recipes and formulas, such questions are always bothersome because there is no one best way. There are, however, many excellent sources of insight. These sources are, as Leo recognized, the people we live and work with.

In an organizational context, a superior constructively pointing out a leader's need for growth can be a great source of insight. The emphasis, of course, is on the word constructive, which means helpful and insightful as opposed to a ceremonial or judgmental appraisal.

Opportunities for honest, constructive feedback from peers and team members can have a similar effect. The leader practiced in the art of self-critique and in the habit of being honest with himself will self-correct. Those who are unable to self-critique find it very nearly impossible to hear the critique of others.

A further source of insight can be perceptive spouses. For example, perceptive wives have unique ways of tugging husbands with distorted self-images back to reality. However, the feedback must be honest and constructive.

The problem, as you have probably recognized by now, is how to make feedback or critique a fundamental part of living and doing business, whether it is self-critique or feedback from others. As mentioned above, there are no formulas, but there are insights which many have found helpful. Before listing those insights, we need to recognize that they fall into two closely related categories: 1) The capacity to solicit and accept constructive feedback and 2) The capacity to provide constructive feedback.

Accepting Constructive Feedback

Our ability to deal responsibly with constructive feedback will often make or break us. No one is 100 percent right 100 percent of the time. We need the reality checks the people around us provide when they believe we value their insight. If the people around us believe we don't want or need their insights, they will often allow us to fail even when they hold in their hand the critical bit of information which might have produced success. Interestingly enough, the insight is usually not withheld because they don't want to help. It is withheld because we have consciously or unconsciously let them know we don't want their feedback.

So, how do we go about building relationships which invite honest, constructive feedback? Here are some insights many have found helpful.

1. **Understand the difference between constructive and destructive feedback.**

    Constructive feedback is usually presented in a positive, helpful, and civil manner. Destructive feedback is frequently negative, sarcastic, and rude. The constructive critic is concerned about issues. The destructive critic wants to focus on personalities. The constructive critic has the best interest of the organization and its people at heart. The destructive critic is driven by a personal, often hidden agenda. Recognizing constructive criticism will help you be more receptive when you are offered feedback.

2. **Don't take yourself too seriously.**

    This includes the ability to laugh at yourself although it goes deeper than a healthy sense of humor about one's own fallibility. Others will offer feedback much more willingly if they know the messenger will not be shot. Approach constructive feedback with an open mind which says: "Yes, I have a position on this issue. However, I am willing to be proven wrong or shown a better way."

3. **Look first at the critic, then at the criticism.**

    Is the critic someone who has earned your trust? Is he or she someone who has provided honest, constructive feedback in the past? If the answer to both these questions is "yes," it is a good idea to give the person a thoughtful hearing. After all, adverse criticism from a wise man is more desirable than the enthusiastic approval of a fool.

4. **Check your attitude toward the person providing feedback.**

    A negative, defensive attitude toward the critic can be more destructive than feedback itself. Giving someone the impression that you are more important than they are and therefore do not have to give them a hearing can damage more than the relationship with that one individual. You could, unintentionally, give others the impression you don't really have to listen to them either.

5. **Remember that the very best people are criticized.** This fact has at least three implications: A) The only way to ensure you won't be criticized is to do nothing; B) No matter who you are there is always room for improvement; C) No one is one hundred percent right one hundred percent of the time.

6. **Keep physically and mentally in shape.** Physical and/or mental exhaustion can have a tremendous effect on the way we act and react. Exhaustion distorts the way we see and handle the world around us. When we become overly tired, we become overly critical. The result is that we are less able to handle feedback whether it is constructive or destructive.

7. **Don't just see the critic; see if there's a crowd.** The following story illustrates this point. Mrs. Jones invited a great and well-known violinist to entertain at her afternoon tea. When it was over everyone crowded around the musician, "I've got to be honest with you," said one of the guests, "I think your performance was absolutely terrible." Hearing this criticism, the hostess tried to ease the sting, "Don't pay any attention to him. He doesn't know what he's talking about. He only repeats what he hears."

8. **Concentrate on your mission.** Especially in the face of destructive criticism and sometimes, even in the face of constructive criticism, it is easy to lose sight of our objective. Maintaining a big-picture perspective is critical to remaining focused. It is equally critical in evaluating the feedback we receive. Some things are simply not worth our time or attention. They do not contribute to our objectives, or the objectives of the organization. Constructive feedback, however, may keep us on course.

Providing Constructive Feedback

Responding gracefully to feedback builds strong professional relationships. Superiors, peers, and team members all appreciate the person who values their constructive input. Accepting feedback is only half of the Feedback Loop, though. The other half is the ability to provide constructive feedback. Every team member is both a receiver and sender. In effective teams, feedback flows in at least two directions and, ideally, in an unlimited number of directions. Therefore leaders/team members must develop effective feedback skills.

On the following pages you will discover some helpful insights for sharpening your feedback skills. Effective feedback skills will enhance your participation in the feedback loop.

1. **Check your motive.** The goal of constructive feedback is to help. Feedback which has a hidden agenda such as settling a score or punishing another will not bring about a positive change in behavior. Two questions will assist you in checking your motives. One, is the feedback motivated by personal or business considerations? If the answer is "business," mentally list the organizational issues you are concerned about. If you cannot list specific concerns, chances are you are acting out of the wrong motive. Two, am I out to make myself look better? Cutting another person down in order to make myself look good is the lowest form of self-gratification. It creates more than resentment. It creates animosity.

2. **Self-critique should come first.** Prior to putting others in their place, put yourself in their place. Look at things from the other person's perspective. Given the same situation, would you have done the same? What would you have done differently?

3. **Take care not to undermine the person's self-confidence.** Try to identify at least one area in which you can offer genuine praise before exposing the problem. Avoid all-inclusive statements like, "You always…" or "You never…" Your confidence in the person's ability to solve the problem should be evident.

4. **Be hard on the issue and easy on the person.** Deal with the issue at hand. When feedback becomes a personal attack, you destroy

your credibility. Constructive feedback leaves the person with a clear understanding of the issue and a sense of hope that it can be turned around.

5. **Don't compare one team member with another.** Relate to people as individuals. Asking individuals to beat their personal best is far less threatening than comparisons between team members. Comparisons cause resentment. Resentment almost always creates hostility.

6. **Be specific.** Constructive criticism will often be interpreted as destructive, personal, or petty when it is non-specific. Say exactly what you mean, and provide examples to back up your concerns. Don't beat around the bush. Aim carefully. Shoot straight. Use a rifle, not a shotgun.

7. **Be sure the time is right.** The ideal time to provide feedback is as soon as you become aware of a problem. However, this is not always the best time. Consider what you know about the individual's personal life. Is the person working through some personal issue such as divorce, grief, or illness? What about the amount of feedback they are trying to assimilate? Don't pile one issue upon another. Most people can effectively deal with only one to two issues at a time. The right time to provide feedback is when the person is able to hear it, not necessarily when you are ready to provide it.

8. **Ask for feedback on your feedback.** Once you have shared your concerns, ask the other person to respond. Make sure they heard what you were trying to say. Sometimes, what we believe we said clearly is not what the other person heard. In addition, reach a consensus about a course of action and offer to help. The offer to invest in the person's success is the most convincing evidence that the criticism is constructive, not personal or petty.

Accepting and providing feedback are opposite sides of the same coin—and the coin is self-critique. Leo refused delivery on feedback from others until he recognized the need to self-critique. Granted, Leo is unusual in that he came to this conclusion on his own. Most of us continue to pound our heads against the wall long after it is obvious to others we need to change. Once Leo was willing to self-critique, his ability to accept and provide constructive feedback paved the way for further professional success.

11

Leaders Manage Conflict

A leader is a peacemaker and a coalition builder.

Once upon a time there was a young man who lived in a second story apartment over a fried fish shop. It just so happens that he was a student and that he did not have much money. He had so little money that all he could afford to eat each day was a single bowl of rice. But each day, when he got ready to eat his bowl of rice, he would open all the windows of his second story apartment and allow the aroma of fried fish from the restaurant below to drift upward. And it was almost like he had fish to eat with his bowl of rice.

One day the young man was standing in front of the fried fish shop talking with a friend. He explained that his financial situation only allowed him a single bowl of rice to eat each day, but he opened all the windows of his apartment to allow the smell of the fish to drift upward. It was almost like he had fried fish to eat. As the young man was talking to his friend, the owner of the fried fish shop ran out onto the sidewalk. The owner grabbed the young man by the arm and said, "You can't be smelling the aroma of my fish frying without paying me something. I think I'm owed something for the smell of my fish." The young man looked at him in amazement and said, "You must be kidding. If I had money to pay for the smell, I'd buy the fish." They argued back and forth for a while, the young man insisting he would not pay; the owner of the fried fish shop insisting he should pay.

Finally, the owner of the fried fish shop said, "Okay, if you won't pay me, I'll sue you." And he did and they landed in court. They each explained their position to the judge. The owner of the fried fish shop said, "He's been smelling the aroma of my fish and I feel I'm owed something for it." The young man said, "Judge, if I could afford to pay for the smell, I'd buy the fish." The judge said, "Let me think about it for a moment." He went into his chambers and after about twenty minutes came out. The judge turned to the owner of the fried fish shop and said, "I've decided you're due something for the smell of your fish." Then he turned to the young man and said, "Do you have any money, any money at all?" And the young man said, "Well, I have just these few coins I've been saving to pay my tuition." And the judge said, "Let me have them." So the young man gave them to the judge who took the coins and dropped them several times from one hand to the other. The coins made the kind of tinkling sound that coins make when they bump together. Then the judge handed the coins back to the young man he had taken them from. The owner of the fried fish shop protested. "Judge, I thought you said I was due something for the smell of my fish." And the judge responded, "I did and you've been paid. I've decided that the price of the smell of fish is the sound of his money."

No doubt the owner of the fried fish shop did not get what he wanted. However, he got what most of us get when we attempt to create a win-lose relationship. The owner of the fried fish shop made a common mistake by allowing his disagreement with the young man to become a competition of wills. And when it became a competition of wills, he was determined that it would end in a win-lose. He, the owner of the fried fish shop would be the winner, and the young man would be the loser. The reality is that the best resolution for conflict is for everyone to win. That is, if you want to have a long-term relationship with the person with whom you are in conflict.

Close on the heels of the myth that a win-lose conflict creates a constructive relationship is the belief that I can win because I'm the boss.

The reality is that any time I win a disagreement only because I'm the boss I have, in fact, lost. Over time, conflict has gotten a bad reputation, to be sure. All our lives we've heard messages such as don't fight, love one another, and be nice. As a result, we see conflict as a sign that somebody (usually the other side) is bad or wrong. Therefore, we try to avoid conflict and sometimes simply pretend it doesn't exist. Ironically, this is precisely the attitude that creates more conflict.

While conflict can be painful, it is a natural, even healthy, part of life. That may be difficult to accept, but once you do, you're free from having to blame a conflict on someone (whether yourself or others). Therefore, you are able to manage it more rationally and productively.

Here's what I mean by dealing with conflict. First, minimize the amount of conflict in your life. Certain behaviors attract conflict like a magnet. When you identify and eliminate them, your life can become a whole lot easier. Examples of conflict magnets would be an arrogant attitude, a condescending manner, or an inappropriate aggressiveness. We have to be careful here to separate aggressive behavior from assertive behavior. Assertiveness is a good thing. It means that I will not allow others to control me—I will control me. Aggressiveness, on the other hand, is the desire to control others. Assertiveness does not create conflict. Aggressiveness does create conflict. Any attempt to gain unreasonable or unacceptable control over the will or behavior of another will result in conflict.

Second, minimize the severity of your conflicts. Not every conflict needs to escalate into World War III. Good conflict managers often find easy, painless resolutions to potentially explosive situations. Sometimes things are small, and they should remain small.

Third, it's possible to win more conflicts. This requires a new definition of winning. As mentioned earlier, normally for there to be a winner there also has to be a loser; that's true in sports, politics, and war. But conflict management includes finding a solution by which both sides can win. The downside is that you don't always get one hundred percent of what you want. Remember, however, that under the old win-lose rules, you often got one hundred percent of nothing. The best reward for handling conflicts confidently is the way you feel about yourself. We have a choice in life to have conflicts with other people or with ourselves. People who avoid external conflicts by complying or pretending to be someone they're not usually end up raging with conflict inside. By bringing conflicts out in the open and dealing with them, we develop honest, forthright, and loving relationships with ourselves and others. We turn heat into light. Here are some suggestions for doing just that.

1. **Choose the time and place carefully**. Never, ever initiate a conflict in a public setting or where uninvolved people are present. Also, be careful about confronting people after a hard day, before an event where they have to be at their best (such as a presentation or performance review), when they are dealing with a mistake or a loss, or when they are working under a deadline. Sensitivity to the other person's circumstances is important in any one-on-one communication, but in a conflict, it is critical.

2. **Change behaviors, not people**. There are two directions you can choose in facing a conflict: 1) You can fix the problem or 2) You can fix the blame. The first is by far more productive. If you make it your goal in a conflict to convince the other person that he or she is wrong, you will almost certainly fail. The reality is that you cannot argue someone out of an emotion, and by the time a conflict escalates, it is almost surely an emotional event. How much better it is simply to change that person's negative behavior, and by changing it, demonstrate to them how change is in their best interest. Or over time, lead them to the appropriate conclusion, that is, allow them to discover it for themselves. Here's an example. If you have a typist who consistently misspells words, you may be tempted to point out that good typists would never make these mistakes, a claim that would certainly be right. Two more productive resolutions, however, would be to buy your typist a speller's

dictionary or better yet, buy a word processor that identifies misspelled words. The key is to keep your eye on the solution, not on the problem.

3. **Agree on something**. Restating your agreement on basic goals makes it easier to discuss your disagreements. It reminds both sides that the relationship is solid which instantly minimizes insecurity and defensiveness and sets the stage for cooperation and problem solving. You're on the same side instead of being adversaries. Here are a couple of ways to state your agreement on basic goals. One is, "I'm bringing this up because I believe in you and want you to succeed here. "We agreed that we need to get this project done by the end of the month" also restates a goal.

4. **Use "I" language**. "I" language means stating your case in terms of your own feelings. For instance, instead of telling someone, "You broke our agreement," you would say, "I'm not happy with the way things are going with our agreement." Notice how the first comment, "you" language, naturally leads to defensiveness. It is, after all, an attack. The second statement may not be welcomed by the other person, but it is far more likely to be accepted. Make "I" language your approach even on minor issues. For instance say, "I didn't understand what you said," instead of "You didn't explain that clearly." By keeping your argument to the facts and preventing personal attacks, "I" language serves all three conflict management fronts: it reduces the number of conflicts, minimizes their severity, and leads more easily to winning solutions.

5. **Figure out where you went wrong.** Define how you may have contributed to the conflict and admit it. Difficult as this is, owning up to your mistakes is one of the most important aspects of conflict resolution. Did your rushed directions contribute to your co-workers mishandling of an issue? If so, admit it early on and you'll free the other person to admit his or her part in the problem.

When appropriate, there's no better way to begin a confrontation than to say, "I know I'm partly responsible for this situation."

6. **Criticize with precision**. A lot of conflict is the result of sloppy and vague criticism. Suppose you tell one of your peers, "You're unprofessional." Unless that person knows what you mean by unprofessional, there's not much he or she can do about it except feel bad, resentful, unmotivated, spiteful—you get the picture. How much better it is to point out specifically, "Punctuality is important to me, and you were twenty minutes late this morning and ten minutes late for this appointment." Conversely, when someone gives you vague criticism, ask that it be clarified. "What am I doing that makes you think I'm unprofessional? I'd like to change it." Think about this the next time you tell someone or someone tells you, "You have a bad attitude," "Your performance isn't up to par," or any one of the many vague criticisms that we hear every day.

7. **When someone attacks, agree**. On occasion, you may find yourself dealing with someone whose goal is to hurt you or to embarrass you in public. Trying to find a win-win solution will not work because the goal is to make you lose. In a case like this, some creative sidestepping may be in order. For example, if someone says "Your tie clashes with your suit," your response might be, "You're right, my tie *does* clash with my suit." By refusing to acknowledge the sniper's implicit attack—you don't how to dress, you're unprofessional, you don't belong here, etc., you have deflected it. In fact, your implied message is, "So what?" a response your attacker will rarely counter.

Another way to handle the person who insults in public is to simply look him or her in the eye for a second or so, then move on. Your implied message is, "I heard what you said, and I'm not going to deal with it." Not dealing with it is a right you can exercise most effectively to leave the insult in the sniper's lap where it belongs. Be careful that you don't pretend you didn't hear the insult; that's powerless behavior. Make sure the eye contact is strong and confident before you move on.

8. **Bow out for a while**. Giving yourself time is a good rule of thumb in all conflicts, but it's particularly important in highly emotional situations. Time allows the emotions to cool and enables both sides to move more easily from the blame phase to the solution stage. Imagine that you have discovered to your outrage that a co-worker has overstepped his or her bounds and caused a big problem for you. Instead of confronting your co-worker immediately, force yourself to wait a few hours or even a day. This doesn't mean you shouldn't have a strong confrontation, just that you'll be more effective once the first rush of anger has subsided.

9. **Have more conflicts**. Many people, believing that conflicts are a sign of a major breakdown in a relationship, strive to have conflict-free relationships. It is a good idea to have conflict-free relationships to the extent that you don't want to have destructive conflict. But you do want to have constructive conflict. Avoiding conflict builds resentment either slowly undermining the positive aspects of the relationship or instantly causing a blowup. How much better it is to bring up problems and annoyances, even minor ones, as they occur. Some people may find this behavior odd at first, but they will come to appreciate the result: a relationship where honesty prevails and neither side keeps an account against the other.

10. **Find the third option**. The minute emotions flair, the natural inclination is for both sides to lock into their positions automatically. The goodwill is gone, and the goal is no longer to resolve the conflict: it is to win. This is a critical juncture and how you handle it determines whether you win or lose at managing conflict. The challenge is to break out of the win-lose pattern.

Two married friends of mine tell of the evening when it was the husband's turn to cook. He didn't feel like cooking so he suggested that they go out to dinner. His wife was tired, and she refused. Just as each was getting into how selfish and insensitive the other was, their four-year old daughter suggested having a pizza delivered. End of argument. Creative solutions are often embarrassingly easy to find. Be open to them.

11. **Agree on the future**. Just as it is helpful to keep your conflict focused on the specifics of the problem, it pays to keep the resolution focused on the specific action that will be taken. For instance, your boss confronts you about exceeding your budget on a project. Instead of saying something like, "I'll be more careful next time," you might suggest that you will present weekly budget updates on your next project. Agreeing to this specific course of action, instead of just stating your good intentions, demonstrates your commitment to solving the problem and dramatically decreases the chance of it happening again.

12. **Work it out on paper**. A tool that integrates the principles I've just presented is reproduced below. It's a simple conflict analysis system that I use in some of my seminars. The beauty of the system, as with all good systems, is its simplicity. If you invest the two minutes it takes to complete this, you are far more likely to get positive results in your next conflict.

    A. Describe the results of the other person's negative behavior. Either describe your feelings ("I get angry") or the bottom line effect in terms of time, money, morale, etc. ("It causes us all to miss our deadlines.")

    B. Describe the other person's negative behavior. Remember to focus on the behavior, not the person. ("When you miss your deadlines" or "When you raise your voice," not "When you act like a jerk.") Remember to be specific and nonjudgmental.

C. Make a request. Identify the preferred behavior, and ask the person to use it. ("Would you please be more realistic about your deadlines?")

D. Describe the positive effect of cooperating. This is the benefit to the person if he or she changes the negative behavior. ("I'm sure we could work together a whole lot better.")

E. Describe the negative effect of not cooperating. This is optional. ("I'm going to have to give you a written warning next time you're late.") Be specific about the follow through then, do it. However, don't make promises you can't keep or don't intend to keep.

The owner of the fried fish shop had a narrow view of the world. He believed that in order to receive what he wanted (payment for the smell of the fish) the young man would have to lose, creating a win-lose relationship. His effort resulted in what we all get when we try to win at the expense of another—nothing but bad feelings. Wise leaders know that while it takes effort to fashion a win-win relationship; it is more than worth the effort.

12

Leaders Create Consensus

A leader is a team player who can follow as well as lead.
A leader understands the task of team building.

Once upon a time there were six blind men. The six blind men sat around a table talking about things they would like to see if, in fact, they could see. As they talked, they all agreed that one of the things they had always wanted to see was an elephant. It just so happens that as they came to this agreement, they heard what they believed to be the sound of an elephant outside the house where they were seated. Together, in single file, they got up and went out into the street and began to examine the elephant the only way blind men can examine an elephant—they began to touch the elephant.

One blind man took hold of the elephant's tail and said to himself, "Who would have thought it? An elephant is nothing more than a rope, just a rope." The second took hold of the elephant's massive hind leg and said to himself, "Who would have thought it? An elephant is just a tree trunk, just a great big tree trunk." The third ran his hands along the massive side of the elephant and said to himself, "What a strange animal. An elephant is just a wall, just a big wall." The fourth blind man took hold of the elephant's ear and holding the elephant's ear between his hands said to himself, "Hmm, quite interesting. An elephant is like a carpet, just a carpet you would put on the floor." And then the fifth man took hold of the elephant's tusk and, running his hands along the tusk, thought to himself, "This must be the most unusual animal in the world. It's just a spear, just like any other spear that a soldier would throw in battle." And finally, the sixth man took hold of the elephant's trunk as it wiggled about. He thought to himself, with a bit of humor, "Who would have imagined that an elephant is nothing more than a fat snake."

Having examined the elephant, the six blind men filed back into the house and sat down around the table and began to share their observations. The first blind man said, "I suppose you guys were kind of surprised to find that an elephant is just a rope—a rope like you would use to tie up a bundle of sticks." And the second man said, "I don't know where you were, but the elephant I had hold of was like a tree trunk." And the third one said, "Both of you are wrong. The elephant is like a wall." The fourth one spoke up and said, "I have no idea where you guys were, but the elephant I had hold of was like a carpet, that's all. Just a carpet you would lay out on the floor." And the fifth one said, "It's hard to believe that all four of you could be so wrong. An elephant is like a spear. I suspect everybody knows that, or anyone who had ever touched an elephant anyway." And finally, the sixth man said, "This is interesting. Apparently there were other animals out there. Because the elephant that I examined was nothing like the animal you've described. To me an elephant is just a big fat, wiggling snake."

And so they began to argue, each one in turn pushing his perspective, insisting that he was right and the others were wrong. After a while a sighted friend came by and the blind men called him over. "Come here, we need you to settle an argument for us. We've just examined an elephant and we want to know which one of us is right."

The first one told of his experience, "An elephant is like a rope." The second, "An elephant is like a tree trunk." The third, "An elephant is like a massive wall." The fourth, "An elephant is like a carpet." The fifth, "An elephant is like a spear." And finally, the sixth man insisted that an elephant is "like a fat, wiggling snake." After listening to each of the six blind men's argument as to what an elephant is like, the sighted friend thought for a moment and this was his response. "Individually, you are all wrong. Together, you are all right."

What was true for the six blind men is true for all would-be teams. Different perspectives are both the strength and the weakness of the team. And, as with the six blind men and the elephant, all would-be teams have a choice. Do we find a way to benefit from our different perspectives and insights, or do we falter because of our different perspectives and insights?

Over the years, we have identified the four stages of team development. These are four stages most would-be teams pass through. They are stages which enable the team to benefit from its diversity.

The first stage is the *forming* stage and occurs when individuals are just learning to deal with one another. This is typically a stage in which little work gets done. The second stage is the *storming* stage and this is a time of stress and trial. Here, the terms under which the team will work are being negotiated. The third stage is the *norming* stage. This is the stage in which roles are accepted. The team begins to feel like a team, and relationships become comfortable and spontaneous. Then the fourth and final stage is the *performing* stage. Optimal levels are finally realized—optimal levels of productivity, quality, decision making, and most of all, constructive interaction.

All successful teams go through all four of these stages. Sometimes a team gets lucky and its mix of personalities or the kinds of leadership that emerges among its members brings the group from forming to performing with a minimum of struggle and in record time. But no team goes directly from forming to performing. Struggle and adaptations are not only critical and difficult, but a necessary part of team development. A good place to begin moving your team from one stage to the next with minimal resistance is to identify where the team currently exists. Understanding these four stages often distinguishes successful teams from failed teams.

I. The Forming Stage

Forming is that stage in the team's development when everything is up for grabs. It is a team in the loosest sense of the word. The talent may all be right there in front of you—good engineers, good planners, good production people, good finance staff, but like a drill sergeant surveying his newest platoon on the first day of boot camp, you've never seen such a rag-tag bunch of individuals in all your born days.

Did you ever, as a kid, transfer to a new school? Remember what that first day felt like? Walking to school, you had one burning desire—to fit in. What mattered most was being accepted by all these strangers. They were going to be an important part of your life for the foreseeable future, and you wanted them to like you. That overwhelming need to fit in, meanwhile, was met with a certain naive opposition to adapting. No one wants to run up the white flag, unconditionally surrendering his or her personal identity. We all want to remain ourselves even as we struggle to fit into a group. We want more information on what we've gotten ourselves into. We want to know who's in charge, and what they're likely to require of us. It's exactly the same with being a team member. We don't want to plunge in; we need to know how cold the water is. That is the ambivalent mind-set we bring to joining new teams. One of the signs of a team at the forming stage is an over-weaning politeness, bending over backwards to be pleasant, not to offend, not to ruffle feathers. Everyone has fifteen seconds of self introduction then sits down, eyes darting nervously. This is understandable when you consider that manners are generally instituted to keep strangers from frightening one another. The hand extended in friendship is an ancient way of demonstrating that one is bringing peaceful intentions to the relationship, not a sword or a club.

This eagerness to appear non-threatening is really a key to how threatening the forming stage usually is. People getting together for the first time have all sorts of unanswered questions. Why are we here? What are we supposed to do? Who has power? Will power be shared?

And, along with their questions, people bring their doubts, prejudices, and insecurities to the team as well.

Amid these unsettling feelings, people cast about anxiously for something, anything, to form temporary alliances. It can be something as simple as two people smoking the same brand of cigarettes, a preference for the same vein of humor, or having worked together in the past: anything that a person can use to feel more comfortable in the larger group. Forming, by the way, is the birthplace of the clique.

During the forming stage, potential teammates identify expectations and desired outcomes, agree on the team's purpose, and identify possible resources and skills sets. They get to know each other, begin to bond, evaluate trust levels, and communicate personal needs. The challenge of forming is the challenge of helping a group of people who has no reason to work together to find a reason to work together. Here are some questions which must be answered in the forming stage:

- Why was I asked to participate on this team?

- Whose idea was the formation of this team?

- Why were we formed?

- Who are the other members and what are their strengths?

- How am I going to find out what they're good at and also let them know what I'm good at?

- How large should the team be?

- How and when are we to bring needed resources to the team and get rid of them when they're no longer needed?

People placed in a new role cast about desperately for common ground. All too typically, they settle on the organization and poke fun at the company for bringing them together to begin with. Within moments of being put together, they can be hard at work fashioning a caricature of the company they work for. Like the drawings of teachers that got them in trouble in the fourth grade, the decision to poke fun at the company is the team's first act of consensus. Someone or something must pay the price and serve as the safety valve for the tension in the group just getting together.

In addition to team size and configuration, other issues must be resolved early on. Who owns the team? Does management own us or do we own ourselves? By ownership, we mean commitment. Typically a new group has a weak sense of purpose and, therefore, has a hard time feeling a sense of ownership. In forming, ownership is virtually all management's. But before a team comes full circle, it will reverse that proportion. Team members will feel a bond of commitment so strong that it will have at least a few insecure people in top management scratching their heads. The team must eventually belong to the team, not to management.

One of the greatest dangers of all is that someone in the group, a quick study, will want to push forward too quickly. The quick study may feel that there is no time to waste and much progress to be achieved by sprinting to the finish line, vaulting over storming and norming directly into performing. But there are no short cuts to team development. The most important job now for this team is to orient itself not to build a better rocket or to double productivity. Its job is to orient itself to itself.

II. The Storming Stage

Forming and storming, together, are usually the most time consuming stages of team development. There is a phrase in industrial psychology called the dynamics of storm and stress, and it refers to an exaltation of individual sensibilities. In other words, it is somewhat necessary for people to experience both disagreement and some measure of stress as they learn to understand each other and to work together successfully. This certainly applies to the storming stage. It is the pathway to team building for sure, but it is replete with individual emotion, group conflict, and change. Storming is not for the squeamish. The best that can be said is that it is necessary and it clears the air. Any issues a team fails to settle during storming will surely return later. Unresolved issues may even drag the team, kicking and screaming, to the eye of its own storm.

All teams are tested in the storming phase. Storming always comes as a surprise, no matter how well one prepares for it. The best one can hope for is that it does not drag on forever as a gruesome war of attrition where no faction can win.

Here are some guidelines that teams still in formation need to consider. Leadership is of paramount importance. The leader who allows the new team unlimited time to sort out individual conflicts will not be successful. This may be the time for stepping in, explaining limits, offering suggestions, keeping a lid on the inevitable anarchy. You do not want storming to outgrow the office, spill over into the lunch room, and finally head down the street, torches ablaze, pitchforks poised for an all out riot.

During forming, the leader's role is to provide direction. He or she points out where people are headed until the group can get its own bearings. During storming, the leader continues to direct traffic, but he or she takes on the additional role of the coach—the person who not only defines the destination, but helps with suggestions on how to get there. Coaching is critical because storming is where the most important dimensions of a team are worked out—its goals, its roles, its relationships, and its likely barriers to long-term team success. Together with its goals which the team began establishing during forming, clarifying and implementing these other three elements comprise the entire agenda of teaming. The coach is there to help, not to interfere. It is a delicate tightrope act to perform. Morale may dip to new lows, and hostilities will emerge and demand a response.

One rule which storming team members often try to encourage in each other is the idea that you can say just about anything. This is true, yet it is not true. It is true that each person must feel free to speak. However, sniping, blaming, and belittling remarks are poison, not only to the targeted individual, but also to the sense of trust necessary for the team to function as a whole. When you first see signs of personal poison bubbling to the surface, that's when to call time out. People have work to do. Tormenting one another is not merely wrong, it's destructive to the team's mission.

As with forming, there are questions during storming that the group must answer to make progress. Those questions include the following:

- What are we supposed to accomplish as a team?

- What are our roles and responsibilities as they relate to accomplishing the goal?

- Who do each of get information from?

- To whom does our information go in order to complete our goal?

- Who's in charge? Will that change from day-to-day, from one phase of the team's process to the next?

- How does one adapt to change in leadership?

- How will we arrive at decisions?

- What happens when we fight?

- How do we increase our ability to take risks until we get to the most direct and most creative level?

- How can we focus our strengths to influence activities outside our own team?

- When will we meet and how—large groups, small groups, one-to-one, etc?

- How can we make ourselves more accessible in order to complete our goals in a timely manner?

A team that answers these questions in the early stages of storming will minimize the pain of a necessarily painful process. Remember that storming takes as much time as there are issues in need of resolution. It is not a difficult task for teams made up of like-minded individuals, all design engineers for example. Cross functional teams are, by nature, made up of unlike-minded individuals.

Leaders should understand the signs of storming. Storming is hope mingled with a large dose of fear. During storming, some team members wonder if they are respected by other team members. Some members will be hostile or overzealous. Some will be intimidated. Pulses will race. Sleep will be lost. Jealousy and infighting, competition and polarization are the order of the day. Alliances that seem solid one day come crashing down the next. Some individuals will rush too soon into the caldron and offer to be boiled down into teams. Others will resist membership as if their lives depend on it.

The worst news for leaders is that storming extracts a terrible toll from them personally. Among the many occurrences in midstorm is a rash of blaming that generally trashes leadership at all levels. Suddenly, you're the reason the group can't get itself together. You're the reason deadlines aren't met. You're the reason individuals feel unfulfilled and misunderstood. As team members wrestle with their identity and direction, leaders are led out for judgment, sometimes gagged and bound. I have seen leaders go white knuckled with rage at the accusations trumped up as part of the team's right of passage. "You weren't there when we needed you," is a common refrain. "You only care about yourself," they say. These can be bitter words to a leader who may have lost sleep every night for a year while grappling with how to intervene, or whether to intervene. Like all developmental stages, there is no alternative to riding out the storm. If it is any comfort, I offer solace that what at first sight appears to leaders a personality conflict is nothing of the sort. And that may be the saving grace of storming. It truly is about team formation and only superficially about personalities.

Storming is the stage in which a few people will decide to stonewall. They will show up for work, and they may still communicate with other team members. But if you look closely at their behaviors, it becomes clear that the team at hand is not the team they wanted, so they have decided against being enthusiastic members. Sometimes an entire team graduates from storming except for one individual, yet it finds itself unable to go on to the next stage. The holdout has them all by the shirttail, keeping them in place while storming on. For an individual like this, there are only two sensible options—get with the team or get out. At the same time, the team and the company owe each member a second chance, maybe even a third chance to reconsider and join the team.

The best analogy for storming is that it is like internal combustion. If you place a teaspoon of gasoline on a sidewalk, it quickly disperses, more or less harmlessly. Compressed in an engine cylinder, however, its vaporized particles begin to bounce into one another at supersonic speeds. Ideally, a controlled explosion occurs and a vehicle many thousands of times the weight and size of the teaspoon of fuel begins to move. When that happens with the team, the storm has broken: roles clarify, a team style materializes, the sun returns to the sky, and a calmer, new day dawns for everyone, best of all, for the team.

III. The Norming Stage

With the passing of the storm comes a new alignment and acceptance of roles within the team. The success experienced during the norming stage is a success marked by contradiction. The group becomes stronger as individuals let down their defenses, acknowledge weaknesses, and ask for help from people with compensating strengths. The norming stage is defined by acceptance of the very roles that storming raged against. Relationships that began in the forming stage as superficial events, coincidences of cigarette brands, favorite jokes, and alma maters have the opportunity to deepen during norming. What's more, the group itself can finally be said to have a relationship with itself. It can show affection for individual members in the storm of banter and rep-artee and genuine consideration. During norming, the ragged edges of conflict begin to subside, tension ebbs, and individuals now poke their heads out like forest creatures after a summer downpour. They realize it is okay to come out of hiding and to be a part of the team.

What has happened is that the hidden agendas covertly advanced by members during storming—"I want to lead," "I want to be left alone," "I deserve the right to disagree on any subject at anytime"—have been unmasked or have diminished in importance. A person's need to assert control over the group, whether actively or passively, shrinks in pro-portion to the growth of knowledge about the group. As the group becomes less threatening, individual members mount fewer threats against it. Even individuals who are still conflicted try to keep conflict from affecting other people's work. People take care not to derail or sabotage the hard-won feeling of team hood the group now enjoys.

As group members become more agreeable, the group as a group gains focus and unity. A splendid dynamic occurs in which every dis-mantled individual defense is used to shore up the group instead. Weaknesses are reconstituted as strengths, information is freely shared, and the group conducts periodic agenda checks to remind itself of its goals and to take note of its progress. During forming, leaders were critical in getting the group going. During storming, leaders were the sacrificial victim as struggling teams groped to achieve consensus at the leader's expense. Now during norming, formal leadership fades as important data is no longer exclusive to leadership. In the next stage, performing, leadership becomes a part of everyone's job and mutual interdependence becomes the order of the day. For the first time, the group may be pictured as a great hulking beast able to move in a single direction, if only haltingly. Before long, the great beast will be doing the dance of dances, the dance that is necessary when people of differ-ent perspectives and different understandings work together success-fully. For the first time, the group will become a true team.

IV. The Performing Stage

There's no guarantee that your team will make it as far as performing. As Hamlet said in his reverie on team playing, "Tis a consummation devoutly to be wished." The work force of America is riddled with teams that never emerge from storming and continue to batter or ignore one another. They may call what they are doing every day from eight to five performing, but the numbers are never there and neither is the feeling. Performing is not "workaholism." In a way, it's the opposite because it is the admission by every member of the team that he or she cannot do the job alone. This is a level of genuine commitment to company goals and objectives, and it may be new to individual team members. Workaholics work every weekend and think they are indispensable because the rest of the world are morons. Therefore, workaholics cannot be part of the team because no one is as competent as they are.

Performers know the real worth of everyone they work with. Performing team members don't get bent out of shape if they're called over the weekend to help solve a pressing problem. Performing means being sufficiently in touch with one's own needs and requirements. It means one can fashion a work schedule that assures progress on team projects without twisting one's own priorities beyond recognition. Performing is a time of great personal growth among team members. With the sharing of the experiences, feelings, and ideas of other team members comes a new level of conscientiousness. It is the sense of knowing where other team members are, a sense of fierce loyalty, even to members who may not be friendly, and the willingness to find a way through any challenge that arises.

Performing means that the team becomes fly-eyed—seeing with many eyes instead of two just as the six blind men were able to see with six different touches or perspectives. This means a reduction in blind spots. It means that the team encountering an elephant, even if the team is blindfolded, will be able to identify exactly what it is, an elephant.

Performing means caring. With performing, members may move beyond the locker room banter of playful teasing into a dimension of communicating that is less self conscious and less afraid. The humor may linger on, but the little missiles we fire at one another throughout the work day will be disarmed or even go away altogether. The humor reflects a lesser degree of veiled aggression and a greater degree of caring. Conflict does not filter into the upper atmosphere during performing; it is more in evidence than ever. Perhaps it is because conflict is put on the table and not reshuffled into the deck that performing works so well. Disagreements are confronted, discussed, considered, and adjudicated.

What seemed destructive during storming (people at odds over projects and turf) seems to be healthy and positive during performing. Once the argument is resolved, team members resume working together. Losing an argument doesn't mean you get roasted. Winning doesn't mean you get to scorch the loser. The order of the day during performing is a good clean fight. The atmosphere is one of enthusiasm and esprit de corps. Best of all, the team is going strong and deadlines are being met. Production is up to par. And, the speed of information flow defies the usual mechanism of memo routing, weekly meetings, and quality checks. People are getting their work done properly on time and in coordinated sequence. And the word goes out throughout the company: "They're onto something over in department X—something called team work."

The Role of the Leader

Forming, storming, norming, and performing are, as I have indicated, an inevitable part of the team building process. The question often asked about these stages is this: What is the role of the leader? The answer is that the leader must be, throughout the process, an adult. The leader is the center of gravity for everyone else who is willing to do the right thing, not only for individual team members, but for the team as a whole. Thus, it is critical for the leader to be an individual who is focused first and foremost on modeling desired behaviors. The leader must provide an example for all in the way he or she manages his or her own behavior. This will establish a foundation of trust. The team leader must seek to be, whether it is acknowledged or not, an extraordinarily trustworthy individual. Thus the question arises: How does a leader build trust? First, the leader must trust others, a critical step during each stage of forming, storming, norming, and performing. Beyond that, here are some steps that a leader can take to demonstrate trust in others.

1. **Spend time with your team**. It's important to spend time with your people if you don't accomplish anything other than being present to talk about what's going on with their families or with their favorite sports team.

2. **Listen to your people without judgment or critique**. Just give people a good listening to. Don't give them a good talking to.

3. **Permit others to influence your decisions rather than dismissing their opinions**. When someone shares what is clearly a good idea, thank them for it. Integrate it into what you're doing.

4. **Reveal and share relevant information with your people.** Let them know everything they need to know and more. Begin with the assumption that all information should be shared unless there is some self-evident reason why information should not be shared.

5. **Be willing to depend on your people rather than keeping total control in your hands**. Don't be a workaholic. Let your people know that just as they need the team to be successful, you need the team to be successful as well.

6. **Give the complex a common sense edge**. Do all that is within your power to make what may seem like a fairly complex process

or idea quite simple. You can often give an issue a common sense edge if, in fact, it is realistic or practical. And if it cannot be given a common sense edge, it may be one indication that it is not practical or reasonable.

7. **Teach your people**. Engage in a process of sharing both your knowledge and experience in a non-threatening manner.

8. **Ask your people to help you identify obstacles to their success and then remove those obstacles quickly**. When an obstacle cannot be removed, be sure to explain why.

These eight steps are an important center of gravity for the leader who would be trusting and trustworthy through each of the four stages. It is essential that the leader be trusting and trustworthy in the forming, storming, norming, and performing stages of team development. It is critical that leaders establish trustworthiness by leading themselves well.

13

My Leader's Code

Once upon a time there were three stonecutters in a large courtyard, each cutting stones with a chisel. A stranger wandered up to them and asked what they were doing. The first one replied curtly, "Can't you see? I'm cutting stones." The stranger quickly moved away and approached the second stonecutter. He again asked, "What are you doing?" The second man replied warmly, "I'm working so that my family can live and grow." The stranger then queried the third cutter, who replied with a swelling sense of pride, "I'm building a cathedral. Each stone I cut goes into a house of worship that will last far beyond my lifetime."

Each worker performed the same task, but how very different the work felt to each of them. The first man felt tired, exhausted, and bored by his work because he was unable to see the larger picture. The second man felt satisfaction, even enthusiasm, because he could see what his work would bring to the people he cared about. The third stonecutter saw his work connected to a larger whole, full of spiritual meaning and significance. His mundane task was energized by a vision of what his stones would become and how they would enrich other people's lives. This cutter was connected to his inner mission with a vision of why he was working.

All the previous chapters of this book have been a preparation for asking the following questions: Which of the three stonecutters are you most like at present, and which of the three matches the inner vision you have for your life in your best moments? What is the personal meaning of your own work? What comes to mind when you think about the vision you have for your life? Are you just a teacher, or are you one who touches the future? Are you just an engineer, or are you one who builds roads which enhance the safety of others? Are you just a cook, or are you one who provides nourishing food for the well-being of others?

People who follow a dream or have a deep sense of purpose about their work are rewarded with an almost inexhaustible supply of energy. They use this energy to reach their goals and to enrich their lives and the lives of others. Such people understand that the future is not a gift; it is an achievement. They know that when you add up a person's yesterdays, they always equal a person's today's. Therefore, they work today with a vision of what they want tomorrow to be.

In the following pages you will find a *Gallery of Classic Morals* (Morals are principles to live by—bits of wisdom which help us realize our best self). This gallery of classic morals is divided into six sections, each section identified by one of the segments from the life wheel shown on the following page. Once you made your way through the gallery, follow the paradigm on pages 136–144 and write your own personal mission statement. Look in your heart and select the vision or dream which energizes you to become the stonecutter you can be.

The Life Wheel

ETHICAL

1. **Live your own life.** Lead your own life. Do not allow others to determine your principles or your priorities. Assume full responsibility for where you've been, where you are, and where you are going.

2. **Laugh often, particularly at yourself.** Life is short; time passes quickly. Decide to enjoy the journey.

3. **Define your vision.** Clearly identify what you want your life to have been when you look back on it in the end. Never allow yourself to forget that if you don't know where you are going, you might end up where you are headed.

4. **Look a person in the eye when you shake hands.** Project an image of mutual worth, courtesy and goodwill. Treat others with esteem, courtesy, and goodwill. Insist on being treated with esteem, courtesy and goodwill.

5. **Be a loyal friend, associate, spouse.** Value relationships over professional success. Be there for people in good times and bad.

6. **Merit divine help.** Live an honorable life. Expect God's help only when doing the right thing and after you have demonstrated a willingness to help yourself.

PERSONAL AND FAMILY

1. **Live a balanced life.** Remember, no individuals ever looked back over their life and wished they had spent less time with a spouse, a child or a friend. Work some, play some, laugh some, and rest some every day.

2. **Love your family and friends unconditionally.** Establish high expectations of honesty and achievement, but love them beyond your disappointments and their failures and mistakes.

3. **Explain to your children where and how you are investing your life.** Take your children to work with you occasionally. Give them a sense of your personal pride of workmanship.

4. **When a friend or family member hurts you, assume that they are also hurting...you will be right most of the time.** Look beyond the friend or family member's anger and try to discover what pain or disappointment is behind the behavior. Then, focus on healing the pain or disappointment.

5. **Let your children know you consider it an honor to be their mom or dad.** Listen to your children. Spend time with your children. Respect your children as persons in their own right. Discipline your children in a way that guides but does not demean.

6. **Celebrate your family and friends.** Remember birthdays, anniversaries, graduations, weddings, bar mitzvahs and baptisms. Beyond these, look for opportunities to celebrate the accomplishments of those closest to you. For example, celebrate a home run, an award, or a recital.

SOCIAL

1. **Be honorable and discreet with the life and reputation of another.** Do not allow a careless word or a word spoken in anger to diminish the life of another. Do not steal from others their good name.

2. **Listen to what people don't say.** People are complex. They frequently expect their friends to listen for what is behind the words they speak—tone, emotion, cries for help.

3. **Salute other people's parades.** Enjoy the enjoyment of others. Allow others the sense of satisfaction and achievement you would claim for yourself. Applaud when their parade passes by.

4. **Treat others with courtesy.** Listen attentively. Speak with humility. Wait with patience. Refuse to patronize. Lace your language and actions with sincere expressions of "please" and "thank you."

5. **Respect the conscience of others.** No matter how different a person's life view, if there is consistency in his beliefs, words and actions, he has integrity. Allow others the dignity of being their own persons and living their own life.

6. **Forgive people for being stupid.** Sooner or later the best and brightest do dumb things. It is part and parcel of being human. Forgive others their human failings, as you would have them forgive yours.

MENTAL

1. **Tell yourself the truth.** Mental health requires a dogged commitment to reality. Self-deception is the first step in personal or professional self-destruction.

2. **Maintain intellectual integrity.** Knowing what you know inspires confidence. Knowing what you don't know, and the integrity to admit it, inspires trust.

3. **Invest in a program of life-long learning.** Discipline yourself to read. Know what is going on in the world and its potential impact on your world. Make time for professional seminars. Give wise men and women a thoughtful hearing.

4. **Admit when you are wrong and do it quickly.** Owning up to your mistakes builds credibility. By doing it quickly, you establish a reputation for accepting responsibility for yourself.

5. **Listen more than you speak.** When you know what others are thinking as well as what you are thinking, you have two sources of information. When you know only what you are thinking, you are at a disadvantage.

6. **Focus on what you can do, not on what you cannot do.** Pour your intellectual energy into the problems at hand. Avoid hand-wringing over problems beyond your control.

PHYSICAL

1. **Protect your most valuable asset.** Unless you are independently wealthy, your greatest financial asset is your capacity to work. Protect your health. Protect your most valuable asset.

2. **Rest and begin again.** The most responsible thing a tired person can do is rest. Exhausted people rarely bring significant change to their world or the world of others.

3. **Listen to your body.** When something about your physiology does not feel right, check it out. Most diseases or injuries can be cured or healed when detected early.

4. **Practice safe living.** Wear safety belts. Buy cars with air bags. Approach stairs with caution. Respect electricity, especially lightning. When a sign says "warning" or "caution," act accordingly.

5. **Play often.** Having fun renews the body, the mind and the soul. Find something which restores your sense of joy and do it often.

6. **Be quiet and still.** Make time to keep in touch with yourself by being still and quiet. The world around you has its own agenda. Only you can protect your vision. Personal moments of stillness and quiet are your best strategy.

FINANCIAL AND PROFESSIONAL

1. **Begin with the end in mind.** Focus on the big picture. Financial and professional success is never a single event. Keep your eye on your destination. Do not allow any single event or person to sidetrack your vision.

2. **Know your strengths and weaknesses.** No one person can know everything. No one person is good at everything. If you need help managing your money, get help. When you need assistance in resolving a professional concern, ask for help. Asking for help is a sign of wisdom and strength.

3. **Don't burn bridges.** Conduct yourself with integrity and grace. You never know what past actions will come back to haunt you.

4. **Disagree without being disagreeable.** Feedback and competing views are essentials of personal and organizational life. After all, no one is 100 percent right 100 percent of the time. How you present your views will determine how you are perceived by others.

5. **Make requests rather than issuing orders.** Unless you are in the military, orders are not usually well received. People want to be asked. A request invites participation and strengthens collegiality.

6. **Invest in the success of others.** Long-term success is almost always the result of win-win partnerships built over a long period of time.

A PARADIGM
FOR DEVELOPING
A PERSONAL MISSION STATEMENT

Follow these suggested steps and you will be able to write a **Personal Mission Statement** that will inspire you and will provide direction for your life. As you work though the paradigm, keep in mind that a Personal Mission Statement is as much a journey as a creation. Don't rush it or set rigid timetables for yourself; rather, work consistently through the paradigm, ask yourself the right questions, and think deeply about your dreams and aspirations.

A meaningful Personal Mission Statement contains two essential elements.

The first element is what you want to accomplish—what your goals are, what contributions you want to make.

The second element is how you would like to be remembered by family, friends and associates—what character strengths you want to have, what virtues you want to develop.

Step One
Define what you want to accomplish and be remembered for.

Some of the elements I would like to have in my Personal Mission Statement are:

What I'd like to accomplish: *What I'd like to be remembered for:*

_____   _____

_____   _____

_____   _____

_____   _____

_____   _____

_____   _____

_____   _____

_____   _____

_____   _____

_____   _____

_____   _____

_____   _____

_____   _____

_____   _____

Step Two
Identify an influential person.

To help you focus on what you want to accomplish and be remembered for, identify an influential individual in your life. This person may be a parent, a work associate, a friend, family member, or neighbor. Answer the following questions, keeping in mind the personal goals you want to accomplish and be remembered for.

Who has been one of the most influential people in my life?

_____

_____

_____

Which of his or her qualities do I most admire?

_____

_____

_____

What qualities have I gained (or hope to gain) from that person?

_____

_____

_____

Step Three
Define your life roles.

You live your life in terms of roles—not in the sense of role-playing—but in the sense of authentic parts you have chosen to fill. You may have roles in work, in the family, in the community, and in other areas of your life. These roles become a natural framework to give order to what you want to accomplish.

You may define your family role as simply family member. Or, you may choose to divide it into roles such as wife and mother or husband and father. Some areas of your life, such as your profession, may involve several roles. For example, you may have one role in administration, one in marketing, and one in long-range planning.

<u>EXAMPLES</u>
Wife/Mother; Manager, New Products; Manager, Research; Manager, Staff Development; United Way Chairperson; Friend.

Husband/Father, Sales Manager, Budget Administration, Sunday School Teacher, Friend.

Define up to six life roles and then write these roles in the boxes provided. Next, project yourself forward in time and write a brief statement of what you would most like to accomplish and be remembered for in each particular role.

By identifying your life role you will gain perspective and balance. By writing these descriptive statements you will visualize what you want to accomplish and how you want to be remembered. You will also identify the core principles and values you want to live by.

Role	Statement
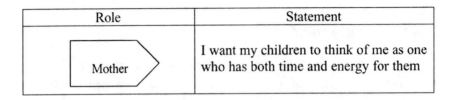 Mother	I want my children to think of me as one who has both time and energy for them

My Life Roles

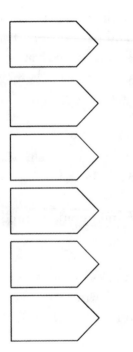

Step Four
Write a draft of your Personal Mission Statement

Now that you have identified your life roles and have defined what you want to accomplish, you are prepared to begin working on your Personal Mission Statement.

In the space provided below write a rough draft of your Personal Mission Statement. Draw heavily upon the thinking you've done in the previous three steps. Carry this draft with you and make notes, additions, and deletions before you attempt another draft.

Step Five
Evaluate

It is important that you keep your Personal Mission Statement up to date. Periodic review and evaluation can help you keep in touch with your own development and keep your statement in harmony with your dreams. Ask yourself these questions on a regular basis:

Is my personal mission based on timeless, proven principles? Which ones?

_____

_____

_____

_____

_____

Do I feel this represents my best?

_____

_____

_____

_____

_____

During my best moments, do I feel good about what this statement represents?

_____

_____

_____

_____

_____

Do I feel direction, purpose, challenge, and motivation when I review this statement?

_____

_____

_____

_____

_____

Which strategies and skills will help me accomplish what I have written?

_____

_____

_____

_____

_____

What do I need to start doing now to be where I want to be tomorrow?

_____

_____

_____

_____

_____

Step Six
Write a final draft

I recommend that you keep a rough draft of your Personal Mission Statement for a while to revise and evaluate. Be sure it inspires the best within you.

When you do have a final copy, review it frequently. I strongly recommend that you commit it to memory and display it prominently so that you keep your vision and your values clearly in mind.

The Next Level:
New Economic Realities

In the past few decades there have been major developments in the national and global economy. These developments have made a high level of self-esteem more urgent for everyone, from the leader of an enterprise to entry-level personnel. The following examples illustrate key developments affecting economic progress:

- The shift from a manufacturing to an information economy entailing the diminishing need for manual or blue-collar workers and the rapidly growing need for knowledge workers with advanced verbal, mathematical, and social skills.

- The escalating explosion of new knowledge, new technology, and new products and services, all of which keep raising the requirements of economic viability.

- The emergence of a global economy of unprecedented competitiveness, yet another challenge to our ingenuity and belief in ourselves.

- The increasing requirement at every level of a business enterprise, not just at the top, but throughout the system, for self-management, personal responsibility, self-direction, and a commitment to innovation and contribution.

- The rise of the entrepreneurial model as central to our thinking about economic adaptiveness.

- The emergence of the mind as the dominant force in all economic activity.

In an agricultural economy, wealth is identified with land. In a manufacturing economy, it is identified with the ability to make things: capital assets and equipment, machines, and various materials used in industrial production. In either of these societies, wealth is understood in terms of matter, not mind; physical assets, not knowledge and information. Intelligence is the guiding force behind economic progress in a manufacturing society, to be sure, but when people think of wealth they think of raw materials such as nickel and copper, and physical property, such as steel mills and textile looms. Wealth is created by transforming the materials of nature to serve human purposes—transforming a seed into a harvest, transforming a waterfall into a source of electricity; transforming iron ore into steel; and transforming steel into the girders of apartment buildings.

If all wealth is the product of mind and labor, of thought directing action, then one way to understand the transition from an agricultural to an industrial society is to say that the balance between mind and physical effort is profoundly altered. Physical labor begins to slide along a declining arc of importance, while mind begins to climb. As an extension of human intelligence, a machine substitutes the power of thought for the power of muscles. Machines make physical labor less demanding and more productive. As technology evolves, the ratio shifts in favor of mind. And as mind becomes more important, self esteem becomes more important.

The climax of this process of development is the emergence of an information economy in which material resources mean less and less, while knowledge and new ideas account for almost everything. The value of a computer, for instance, lies not in its material components, but in its design—in the thinking and knowledge it embodies—and in the quantity of human effort it makes unnecessary. Microchips are made out of sand; their value is a function of the intelligence encoded within them. A copper wire can carry forty-eight telephone conversations; a single fiber-optic cable can carry more than eight thousand conversations. Yet fiber-optic cables are cheaper, more efficient, and much less energy consuming to produce than copper.

Each year since 1979, the United States has produced more with less energy than the year before. The worldwide drop in the price of raw materials is a consequence of the ascendancy of mind in our economic life. The mind always has been our basic tool of survival. For most of our history, this fact has not been understood. Today it is obvious.

In an economy in which knowledge, information, and creativity—and their translation into innovation—are clearly the source of wealth and competitive advantage, there are distinct challenges both to individuals and to organizations.

Individuals, whether employees or self-employed professionals, face the following challenges:

- Acquiring appropriate knowledge and skills and committing oneself to a lifetime of continuous learning made mandatory by the rapid growth of knowledge.

- Working effectively with other human beings: developing written and oral communication skills, participating in non-adversarial relationships, building consensus through give and take, and being willing to assume leadership and motivate co-workers.

- Managing change and responding appropriately.

- Cultivating the ability to think for oneself—for without this ability, innovativeness is impossible.

Such challenges entail the need to bring a high level of consciousness to one's work. This consciousness demands the acquisition of knowledge and skill and to provide opportunities for growth and self-development. A commitment to life-long learning is a natural expression of the practice of living consciously.

In relating to other people, one needs the self-respect that underlies respect for others; freedom from gratuitous fear, envy, or hostility; the expectation of being dealt with fairly and decently; and the conviction that one has genuine value to contribute. Again we are led to the importance of self-esteem. Moreover, the success of cooperative endeavors rests on the willingness of participants to be accountable, a corollary of the practice of self-responsibility. Such endeavors rely on the willingness of people to keep their promises, honor their commitments, think about the consequence of their actions on others, and manifest reliability and trustworthiness—all expressions of the practice of personal integrity. Self-esteem is far from being the only asset one needs—let there be no mistake about this—but without it one is severely impaired and is, in effect, at a competitive disadvantage.

To organizations, the challenges include the following:

• Responding to the need for a constant stream of innovation by cultivating a discipline of innovation and entrepreneurship into the mission, strategies, policies, practices, and reward system of the organization.

• Designing a culture in which initiative, creativity, self-responsibility, and contribution are fostered and rewarded.

• Recognizing the relationship between self-esteem and performance. Implementing policies that support self-esteem is a challenge that demands recognizing and responding to the employees' need for a sane, intelligible, non-contradictory environment that a mind can make sense of; for learning and growth; for achievement; for being listened to and respected; for being allowed to make responsible mistakes.

When prospective employees ask themselves, "Is this an organization where I can learn, grow, develop, and enjoy my work?" they are implicitly asking, whether they recognize it or not, "Is this a place that supports my self-worth or a place that injures it?"

Conditions of a High Self-Esteem Organization

An organization whose people operate at a high level of consciousness, self-acceptance (and acceptance of others) self-responsibility, self-assertiveness (and respect for the assertiveness of others), purposefulness, and personal integrity will be an organization of extraordinarily empowered human beings. These traits are supported in an organization to the extent that the following conditions are met:

- *People feel safe:* They are secure that they will not be ridiculed, demeaned, humiliated, or punished for openness and honesty or for admitting, "I made a mistake" or for saying, "I don't know, but I'll find out."

- *People feel accepted:* They are treated with courtesy, listened to, invited to express thoughts and feelings, and dealt with as individuals whose dignity is important.

- *People feel challenged:* They are given assignments that excite, inspire, test and stretch their abilities.

- *People feel recognized:* They are acknowledged for their individual talents and achievements and rewarded monetarily and non-monetarily for extraordinary contributions.

- *People receive constructive feedback:* They hear how they can improve performance in non-demeaning ways that stress positives rather than negatives and build on their strengths.

- *People see that innovation is expected:* Opinions are solicited, brainstorming is invited, and new ideas are welcomed.

- *People are given easy access to information:* Not only are they given the information (and resources) they need to do their job properly, they are also given the wider context in which they work—the company's goals and progress—so they can understand how their work relates to the organization's overall mission.

- *People are given authority appropriate to their accountability:* They are encouraged to take initiative, make decisions, and exercise judgment.

- *People are given clear-cut and non-contradictory rules and guidelines:* They are provided with a structure their intelligence can grasp and rely on, and they know what is expected of them.

- *People are encouraged to solve their own problems:* They are expected to resolve issues close to the action rather than pass responsibility for solutions to higher-ups—and they are empowered to do so.

- *People see that rewards for success are far greater than any penalties for failure:* Too many companies make the penalties for mistakes much greater than the rewards for success, and people are afraid to take risks or express themselves.

- *People are encouraged to learn and are rewarded for learning:* They are encouraged to participate in internal and external courses and programs that will expand their knowledge and skills.

- *People observe congruence between an organization's mission statement and professed philosophy, on the one hand, and the behavior of leaders and managers on the other:* They see integrity exemplified, and they feel motivated to model what they see.

- *People experience fair and just treatment:* They feel that the workplace is a rational universe they can trust.

- *People take pride in the value of what they produce:* They perceive the result of their efforts as genuinely useful; they perceive their work as worth doing.

The extent to which these conditions are operative in an organization will be the extent to which an organization is a place where people with high self-esteem will want to work. It will also be one in which people of more modest self-confidence will find their self-confidence increased.

Creating a High Self-Esteem Organization

For leaders who want to build a high-performance/high self-esteem organization, I would structure a different but inevitably overlapping list of proposals that go to the heart of what such an organization requires:

- *Work on your own self-esteem:* Commit yourself to raising the level of consciousness, responsibility, and integrity you bring to your work and your dealings with people—staff, reports, associates, higher-ups, customers, and suppliers.

- *When you talk with your people, be present:* Make eye contact, listen actively, offer appropriate feedback, give the speaker the experience of being heard. Be empathic: let the speaker know that you understand his or her feelings as well as statements—which is a way of giving the speaker an experience of being visible.

- *No matter who you are speaking to, maintain a tone of respect:* Do not permit yourself to speak in a condescending, superior, sarcastic, or blaming tone.

- *Keep work encounters task-centered, not ego-centered:* Never permit a dispute to deteriorate into a conflict of personalities. The focus needs to be on reality. What is the situation? What does the work require? What needs to be done?

- *Give your people opportunities to practice self-responsibility:* Give them space to take the initiative, volunteer ideas, attempt new tasks, and expand their range.

- *Speak to your people's understanding:* Give reasons for rules and guidelines (when they are not self-evident); explain why you cannot accommodate certain requests; do not merely hand down orders from on high.

- *If you make a mistake in your dealings with someone, if you are unfair or short-tempered, admit it and apologize:* Do not imagine (like an autocratic parent) that it will demean your dignity to admit taking an action you now regret.

- *Invite your people to give you feedback on the kind of leader you are:* I agree with someone who once said, "You are the kind of leader your people say you are." So check it out, and let your people see that you are open to learning and self-correction. Set an example of non-defensiveness.

- *Let your people see that it is safe to make a mistake or say "I don't know, but I will find out:"* To evoke fear of error or ignorance is to invite deception, inhibition, and an end to creativity.

- *Let your people see that it is safe to disagree with you:* Convey respect for differences of opinion. Do not punish those who disagree

- *Describe undesirable behavior without blaming:* Let someone know if his or her behavior is unacceptable, communicate consequences and what kind of behavior is expected, and refrain from character assassination.

- *Let your people see you talk honestly about your feelings:* When you are hurt or angry or offended, say so with honesty and dignity and give everyone a lesson in the strength of self-acceptance.

- *If someone does superior work or makes an excellent decision, invite him or her to explore how it happened:* Do not limit yourself simply to praise. By asking appropriate questions, help raise the person's consciousness about what made the achievement possible, and thereby increase the likelihood that they will repeat the behavior in the future.

- *If someone does unacceptable work or makes a bad decision, practice the fore-going principle:* Do not limit yourself to corrective feedback. Invite an exploration of what made the error possible, thus raising the level of consciousness and minimizing the likelihood of repetition.

- *Provide clear and unequivocal performance standards:* Let people understand your nonnegotiable expectations regarding the quality of work.

- *Praise in public and correct in private:* Acknowledge achievements within the hearing of as many people as possible while letting a person absorb corrections in the safety of privacy.

- *Let your praise be realistic:* Like parents who praise their children's every accomplishment extravagantly, you weaken your positive acknowledgments if they are not calibrated to the reality of what has been accomplished.

- *When someone's behavior creates a problem, ask him or her to propose a solution:* Avoid handing down solutions. Give the problem to the responsible party, thereby encouraging responsibility, self-assertiveness, and self-awareness. ˙

- *Convey in every way possible that you are not interested in blaming—you are interested in solutions—and exemplify this policy personally:* When we look for solutions, we grow in self-esteem; when we blame (or alibi), we weaken others' self-esteem.

- *Give your people the resources, information, and authority to do what you have asked them to do:* Remember that there can be no responsibility without power, and nothing so undermines morale as assigning the first without giving the second.

- *Remember that a great leader is not one who comes up with brilliant solutions, but one who sees to it that his people come up with brilliant solutions:* A leader, at his or her best, is a coach, not a problem solver for admiring children.

- *Take personal responsibility for creating a culture of self-esteem:* No matter what is said, reports are unlikely to sustain the kind of behavior I am recommending if they do not see it exemplified by higher ups.

- *Change aspects of the organization's culture that undermine self-worth:* Avoid over-directing, over-observing, and over-reporting. Excessive managing (micro-managing) is the enemy of autonomy and creativity.

- *Plan and budget appropriately for innovation:* Do not ask for people's innovative best and then announce there is no money (or other resources)—creative enthusiasm may dry up and be replaced by low morale.

- *Ask your people what they need in order to feel in control of their work, and if possible, give it to them:* To promote autonomy, excitement, and a strong commitment to goals—empower, empower, empower.

- *Stretch your people's abilities:* Assign tasks and projects slightly beyond their known capabilities.

- *Educate your people to see problems as challenges and opportunities:* This perspective is clearly shared by high achievers and people with high self-confidence.

- *Support the talented individualist:* In addition to the necessity for effective teamwork, there should be a place for the brilliant hermit who moves to different music; team players benefit from this respect for individuality.

- *Teach that mistakes are opportunities for learning:* "What can you learn from what happened?" is a question that promotes self-worth; it also prevents repeating mistakes, and sometimes it points the way to a future solution.

- *Challenge the seniority tradition, and promote from any level on the basis of merit:* Recognition of ability inspires self-respect.

- *Set a standard of personal integrity:* Keep your promises, honor your commitments, deal with everyone fairly (not just insiders, but suppliers and customers as well), and acknowledge and support this behavior in others; your people will take pride in working for a principled leader.

I doubt there is one principle listed here that thoughtful leaders are not already aware of—in the abstract. The challenge is to practice them consistently and weave them into the fabric of daily procedures.

In conclusion, the higher the self-confidence of the leader, the more likely it is that he or she can inspire others. A mind that distrusts itself cannot evoke the best in the minds of others. Nor can leaders inspire the best in others if their primary need arising from their insecurity is to prove themselves right and others wrong.

It is a fallacy to say that a great leader should be egoless. A leader needs an ego sufficiently healthy that it does not feel itself on the line in every encounter—the leader is free to concentrate on tasks and results, not self-promotion or self-protection.

If degrees of self-confidence are placed on a scale from one to ten, with ten representing optimal self-confidence and one the lowest imaginable, then is a leader who is rated a five more likely to hire a seven or a three? Very likely, this leader will feel more comfortable with the three since insecure leaders often feel intimated by others more confident than themselves. Multiply this example hundreds of times and project the consequences for an organization.

Leaders often do not fully recognize the extent "who they are" affects virtually every aspect of their organization. They do not appreciate the extent to which they are role models. Their smallest behaviors are noted and absorbed by those around them, not necessarily consciously, and reflected via those they influence throughout the organization. If a leader has unimpeachable integrity, a standard is set that others feel drawn to follow. If a leader treats people with respect—associates, reports, customers, suppliers, shareholders—that behavior tends to translate into a company culture. For these reasons, a person who wants to develop leadership ability should work on self-confidence as an expression of self-esteem.

Can the right organizational environment transform a person of low self-esteem into one with high self-esteem? Not very likely, although a good leader can establish in a person a foundation for improved self-respect. Clearly there are troubled individuals who need more focused professional help, and it is not the function of a business organization to be a psychological clinic. For the person of average self-esteem, an organization dedicated to the importance of the individual has immense potential for doing good at the most intimate and personal level—even though that is not, of course, its purpose for being. And in doing so, it contributes to its own life and vitality in ways that are not remote and ethereal but, ultimately, bottom line.

The policies that support self-esteem are also the policies that make money. The policies that demean self-esteem are the policies that sooner or later cause a company to lose money. When you treat people with disrespect and frustrate ego energy, you cannot possibly hope to get their best. And in today's fiercely competitive, global economy, nothing less than their best is good enough.

The Next Level:
What Is Self-Esteem?

Most of us are children of dysfunctional families. I do not mean that most of us have alcoholic parents or were sexually, physically, or otherwise abused or that we grew up in an atmosphere of physical violence. I mean that most of us grew up in homes characterized by conflicting signals—denials of reality, parental lying, and lack of adequate respect for our mind and person. I am speaking of the average home.

Let me give you an example of the kind of craziness with which so many of us grew up. Imagine a scene involving a child, a mom, and a dad. Seeing a look of unhappiness on the mom's face, the child asks, "What's the matter, mommy? You look sad." Mom answers, her voice tight and tense, "Nothing is the matter. I'm fine." Then dad says angrily, "Don't upset your mother!" The child looks back and forth between mother and father, utterly bewildered. Unable to understand the rebuke, the child begins to cry. The mom cries to the dad, "Now, look what you've done."

I like this story because of its ordinariness. Let's take a closer look at it. The child correctly perceives that something is troubling mother and responds appropriately. Mother acts by invalidating the child's [correct] perception of reality. Mother lies, though you could argue that was not her intention. Perhaps mother does so out of the misguided desire to "protect" her child, or perhaps she herself does not know how to handle her unhappiness.

If she had said "Yes, mommy is feeling a little sad right now, thank you for noticing," she would have validated the child's perception. By acknowledging her own unhappiness, simply and openly, she would have reinforced the child's compassion and taught something important concerning a healthy attitude toward pain. She would have taken the catastrophe out of the situation.

Father, perhaps to "protect" the mother or perhaps out of guilt because mother's sadness concerns him, scolds the child, thus adding to the incomprehensibility of the situation. If the mother is not sad, why would a simple inquiry be upsetting? If she is sad, why is it wrong to ask about it and why is mommy lying?

Now to confound the child still more, mother screams at father, rebuking him for reproaching their child. Contradictions compound and incongruities mount. How is the child to make sense out of this situation?

The child may run outside, frantically looking for something to do or someone to play with, seeking to erase all memory of the incident as quickly as possible, repressing feelings and perceptions. And if the child flees into unconsciousness to escape the terrifying sense of being trapped in a nightmare, do we blame her well-meaning parents for behaving in ways that encourage her to feel that sight is dangerous and that there is safety in blindness?

A Story Without Villains

No one is likely to imagine that the parents are motivated by destructive intentions. But in choosing to deny simple reality, they give the child the impression that she exists in an incomprehensible world where perception is untrustworthy and thought is futile. Multiply that incident by a thousand, more or less like it, none of which the child is likely to remember in later years, but all of which will almost certainly have a cumulative impact on the child's development.

If the child does draw the conclusion that her mind is powerless, how can a good self-esteem develop? And without it, how can she face life?

Complex Factors Determine Our Self-Esteem

I do not wish to imply that how our parents treat us determines the level of our self-esteem. The matter is more complex than that. We have a decisive role of our own to play. The notion that we are merely pawns, shaped and determined by our environment, cannot be supported scientifically or philosophically. We are all causal agents in our own right, active contestants in the drama of our lives, originators and not merely reactors or responders.

Clearly, however, the family environment can have a profound impact for good or for ill. Parents can nurture self-trust and self-respect, or place appalling roadblocks in the way of learning such attitudes. They can convey that they believe in their child's competence and goodness, or they can convey the opposite.

They can create an environment in which the child feels safe and secure or they can create an environment of terror. They can support the emergence of healthy self-esteem, or they can do everything conceivable to subvert it.

Obstacles to the Growth of Self-Esteem

Parents throw up severe obstacles to the growth of a child's self-esteem in the following ways:

1. Convey that the child is not "enough."

2. Chastise the child for expressing "unacceptable" feelings.

3. Ridicule or humiliate the child.

4. Convey that the child's thoughts and feelings have no value or importance.

5. Attempt to control the child by shame or guilt.

6. Overprotect the child and consequently, obstruct normal learning and increase age appropriate self-reliance.

7. Raise the child with no rules at all, and thus, no supporting structure. Or else, institute rules that are contradictory, bewildering, un-discussable, and oppressive. In any case, inhibiting normal growth.

8. Deny a child's perception of reality and implicitly encouraging the child to doubt his or her mind.

9. Treat evident facts as unreal, thus shaking the child's sense of rationality. For example, when an alcoholic father stumbles to the dinner table, misses the chair, and falls to the floor as the mother goes on eating or talking as if nothing has happened.

10. Terrorize a child with physical violence or the threat of it, thus instilling acute fear as an enduring characteristic at the child's core.

11. Treat a child as a sexual object.

12. Teach that the child is bad, unworthy, or sinful by nature.

Today, millions of men and women who have come out of such childhood experiences are searching for ways to heal their wounds. They recognize that they have entered adult life with a liability, a deficit of self-esteem.

Whatever words they use to describe the problem, they know they suffer from some nameless sense of not being "enough" or some haunting emotion of shame or guilt or of generalized self-distrust or a diffusive feeling of unworthiness. They sense their lack even if they do not know precisely what self-esteem is, let alone, how to nurture and strengthen it within themselves.

A Definition of Self-Esteem

As teachers and parents, we seek to fan a spark in those we work with and seek to raise, that innate sense of self-worth that presumably is our human birthright. But that spark is only the anteroom to self-esteem. If we are to do justice to those we work with and we seek to raise, we need to help them develop that sense of self-worth into the full experience of self-esteem.

Self-esteem is the experience that we are equipped for life and the requirements of life. More specifically, self-esteem is characterized by these two qualities:

1. Confidence in our ability to think and cope with the challenges of life.

2. Confidence in our right to be happy, the feeling of being worthy, deserving, entitled to assert our needs and wants, and to enjoy the fruits of our efforts.

A Powerful Human Need

Self-esteem is a powerful human need. It is a basic human need that makes an essential contribution to the life process. It is indispensable to normal and healthy development. It has survival value.

Lacking positive self-esteem, our psychological growth is stunted. Positive self-esteem operates as, in effect, the immune system of consciousness, providing resistance, strength, and a capacity for regeneration.

When self-esteem is low, our resilience in the face of life's adversities is diminished. We crumble before life's challenges, challenges that a healthier sense of self could vanquish. We tend to be more influenced by the desire to avoid pain, than to experience joy. Negatives have more power over us than positives.

Addiction and Self-Esteem

These observations help us to understand addictions. We either become addicted to alcohol, drugs, or destructive relationships, with conscious inattention invariably to ameliorate anxiety and pain. What we become addicted to are tranquilizers and anything that can ease our pain. The "enemies" we are trying to escape are fear and pain. When the means we have chosen do not work and make the problems worse, we are driven to take more and more of the poison that will eventually kill us.

Addicts are not less fearful than other human beings. They are more fearful. The pain is not milder, it is more severe. We cannot drink or drug our way into self-esteem any more than we can buy happiness with toxic relationships. We do not attain self-esteem by practices that evoke self-hatred. If we do not believe in ourselves, neither in our efficacy nor in our goodness, the universe is a very frightening place.

Valuing Ourselves

This does not mean that we are necessarily incapable of achieving any real values. Some of us may have the talent and drive to achieve a great deal in spite of a poor self-concept. Like the highly productive workaholic who is driven to prove his worth, to a father who predicted he would amount to nothing.

But it does mean that we will be less effective, less creative than we have the power to be and it means that we will be crippled in our ability to find joy in our achievements. Nothing we do will ever feel like "enough."

If we have realistic confidence in our mind and value, if we feel secure within ourselves, we tend to experience the world as open to us and to respond appropriately to the challenges and opportunities. Self-esteem empowers, energizes, motivates. It inspires us to achieve and allows us to take pleasure and pride in our achievements. It allows us to experience satisfaction.

In their enthusiasm, some writers today seem to suggest that a healthy sense of self-value is all we need to assure happiness and success. The matter is far more complex than that. We have more than one need and there is no single solution to all the problems of our existence.

A well-developed sense of self is a necessary condition of our well being, but not a sufficient condition. Its presence does not guarantee fulfillment, but its lack guarantees some measure of anxiety, frustration, or despair.

Self-esteem proclaims itself as a need by virtue of the fact that its [relative] absence impairs our ability to function. This is why we say it has survival value, and never more so than today. We have reached a moment in history when self-esteem, which has always been an extremely important psychological need, has also become a supremely important economic need—an attribute imperative for adaptiveness to an increasingly complex, challenging, changing, and competitive world.

Psychological Resources for the Future

The shift from a manufacturing society to an information society, the shift from physical labor to mind work as the dominant employee activity in the emergence of a global economy characterized by rapid change, accelerated scientific and technological breakthroughs, and an unprecedented level of competitiveness create demands for higher levels of education and training than were required of previous generations. Everyone acquainted with business culture knows this. But what is not equally understood is that these developments also create new demands on our psychological resources. Typically, these developments ask for a greater capacity for innovation, self-management, personal responsibility, and self-direction. This is asked not just "at the top," but also at every level of the corporate enterprise from senior management to first-line supervisors, and even entry-level personnel.

A modern business can no longer be run by a few people who *think* and a great many people who *do* what they are told [the traditional military command and control model]. Today organizations need not only an unprecedently higher level of knowledge and skill among all those who participate, but also a higher level of personal autonomy, self-reliance, self-trust, and the capacity to exercise initiative. In a word, everyone needs higher self-esteem.

This means that people possessing a decent level of self-esteem are now needed economically in large numbers. Historically, this is a new phenomenon.

Intelligent Choices Require Healthy Self-Esteem

In a world where there are more choices and options than ever before, and frontiers of limitless possibilities face us in whatever direction we look, we require a higher level of personal autonomy. This means a greater need to exercise independent judgment, to cultivate our own resources, and to take responsibility for the choices, values, and actions that shape our lives, a greater need for self-trust and self-reliance, and a greater need for a reality-based belief in ourselves.

The greater the number of choices and directions we need to make at a conscious level, the more urgent our need for healthy self-esteem. To the extent that we are confident in the efficacy of our minds, confident of our ability to think, learn, and understand, we tend to persevere when faced with difficulties or complex challenges.

Persevering, we tend to succeed more often than we fail, thus confirming and reinforcing our sense of efficacy. To the extent that we doubt the efficacy of our minds and lack confidence in our thinking, we tend not to persevere, but to give up. Giving up, we fail more often than we succeed, thus confirming and reinforcing our negative self-assessment.

High self-esteem seeks the stimulation of demanding goals and reaching demanding goals nurtures good self-esteem. Low self-esteem seeks the safety of the familiar and undemanding. And confining one-self to the familiar and undemanding serves to weaken self-esteem.

The higher our self-esteem, the better equipped we are to cope with adversity in our careers or in our personal lives. The quicker we are to pick ourselves up after a fall, the more energy we have to begin anew.

The higher our self-esteem, the more ambitious we tend to be. Not necessarily in a career or financial sense, but in terms of what we hope to experience in life emotionally, creatively, even spiritually. The lower our self-esteem, the less we aspire to and the less we are likely to achieve. Either path tends to be self-reinforcing and self-perpetuating. The higher our self-esteem, the more disposed we are to form nourishing rather than toxic relationships.

Like is drawn to like, health is attracted to health, and vitality and expansiveness in others are naturally more appealing to people with good self-esteem than emptiness and dependency.

Attraction to Those Whose Self-Esteem Matches Our Own

An important principle of human relationships is that we tend to feel more comfortable, most "at home" with people whose self-esteem level resembles our own. High self-esteem individuals tend to be drawn to high self-esteem individuals. Medium self-esteem individuals are typically attracted to medium self-esteem individuals. Low self-esteem seeks low self-esteem in others.

The most disastrous relationships are those between two persons, both of whom think poorly of themselves. Predictably, the union of two abysses does not produce a height.

I once knew a woman who grew up feeling she was bad and undeserving of kindness, respect, or happiness. She married a man who "knew" he was unlovable and felt consumed by self-hatred. He protected himself by being cruel to others before they could be cruel to him. She did not complain about his abuse, since she "knew" that abuse was her destiny. He was not surprised by her increasing withdrawal and remoteness from him since he "knew" no one could ever love him.

They had spent twenty years of torture together "proving" how right they were about themselves and about life. When I commented to the wife that she had not known much happiness, she looked astonished and said, "Are people ever really happy?"

The higher our self-esteem, the more inclined we are to treat others with respect, benevolence, goodwill, and fairness since we do not tend to perceive them as a threat and since self-esteem is the foundation of respect for others. It is, after all, simply an expression of the respect we have for ourselves.

The Time Bomb of Poor Self-Esteem

While an inadequate self-esteem can severely limit an individual's aspirations and accomplishments, the consequences of the problem need not be so obvious. Sometimes the consequences show up in more indirect ways.

The time bomb of a poor self-concept may tick silently for years, while an individual, driven by a passion for success and exercising genuine ability may rise higher and higher in his or her profession. Then, without real necessity, he or she starts cutting corners, morally and/or legally in his or her eagerness to provide more lavish demonstrations of their mastery. Then, they commit more flagrant offences still, telling themselves that this is "beyond good and evil" as if challenging the fates to bring them down. Only at the end when life and career explode in disgrace and ruin, can the individual see how for many years they have been moving relentlessly toward the final act of an unconscious life script that they began writing at the age of three.

Self-Efficacy and Self-Respect

Self-respect has two interrelated aspects

1.   A sense of personal efficacy [self-efficacy].

2. A sense of personal worth [self-respect].

As a fully realized psychological experience, self-respect is the integrated sum of these two aspects. Self-efficacy means confidence in the functioning of my mind, in my ability to think, and the processes by which I judge, choose, and decide. It is confidence in my ability to understand the facts of reality that fall within the sphere of my interests and needs, cognitive self-trust, and cognitive self-reliance.

Self-respect means assurance of my value, an affirmative attitude toward my right to live and be happy, comfort in appropriately asserting my thoughts, wants, and needs; the feeling that joy is my natural birthright.

Consider that if an individual felt inadequate to face the challenges of life, if an individual lacked fundamental self-trust, confidence in his or her mind, we would recognize the presence of a self-esteem deficiency, no matter what other assets he or she possessed.

Or, if an individual lacked a basic sense of self-respect, felt unworthy or undeserving of the love and respect of others, unentitled to happiness, fearful of asserting thoughts, wants, or needs again, we would recognize a self-esteem deficiency no matter what other positive attributes he or she exhibited.

The Dual Pillars of Self-Esteem

Self-efficacy and self-respect are the dual pillars of healthy self-esteem. Lacking either one, self-esteem is impaired. They are the defining characteristics of the term because of their fundamentality. They represent not derivative or secondary meanings of self-esteem, but its essence.

The experience of self-efficacy generates the sense of control over one's life that we associate with psychological well being—the sense of being at the vital center of one's existence as contrasted with being a passive spectator and a victim of circumstances.

The experience of self-respect makes possible a benevolent, non-neurotic sense of community with other individuals, fellowship of independence and mutual regard as contrasted with either alienated estrangement from the human race on the one hand, or a mindless submergence into the tribe on the other.

Within a given person, there will be inevitable fluctuations in self-esteem levels, much as there are fluctuations in all psychological states. We need to think in terms of a person's average level of self-esteem.

How Do We Experience Our Self-Esteem

While we sometimes speak of self-esteem as a conviction about oneself, it is more accurate to speak of a disposition to experience oneself a particular way. What way? To recapitulate:

1. As fundamentally competent to cope with the challenges of life, thus trust in one's mind and processes—self-efficacy.

2. As worthy of success and happiness thus the perception of one's self as someone to whom achievement, success, respect, friendship, and love are appropriate—self-respect.

A Formal Definition of Self-Esteem

To sum up in a formal definition, self-esteem is the disposition to experience one's self as competent to take on the challenges of life and deserving of happiness.

Note that this definition does not specify the childhood environmental influences that support healthy self-esteem [for example, physical safety, nurture, etc.], nor the later internal generators [the practice of living conscientiously, self-responsibly], nor emotional or behavioral consequences [compassion, willingness to be accountable, etc.].

It merely identifies what the self-evaluation concerns and consists of. Am I suggesting that the definition of self-esteem I offer is written in stone and can never be improved on? Not at all. Definitions are by nature contextual. They relate to a given level of knowledge. As knowledge grows, definitions typically become more precise.

The concept of "competence" as used in my definition is metaphysical, not "western." That is, it pertains to the very nature of things, to our fundamental relationship to reality. It is not the product of a particular culture. There is no society on earth, no society even conceivable whose members do not face the challenges of fulfilling their needs, who do not face the challenges of appropriate adaptation to nature and to the world of human beings. The idea of efficacy in this fundamental sense [which includes competence in human relationships] is not a "western" idea as I have heard suggested on some occasions. It is, instead, a universal need.

We delude ourselves if we imagine there is any culture or society in which we will not have to face the challenge of making ourselves appropriate to life. Every person in every culture in every part of the world struggles to discover meaning in life. For every single person, that meaning, to some degree, is met through self-esteem.

The Next Level:
Why Do We Need Self-Esteem?

To understand self-esteem, we must ask the following question: Why do we need self-esteem? For lower animals, the question of the efficacy of their consciousness or the worthiness of their being does not exist. Only human beings wonder: Can I trust my mind? Am I competent to think? Am I adequate? Am I enough? Am I a good person? Do I have integrity; that is, is there congruence between my ideals and my practice? Am I worthy of respect, love, success, and happiness?

It is not self-evident why such questions should even occur. Our need of self-esteem is the result of two basic facts, both intrinsic to the human experience.

The first is that we depend for our survival and our successful mastery of the environment on the appropriate use of our consciousness. Our lives and well-being depend on our ability to think.

The second is the right use of our consciousness is not automatic. It is not "hard wired" by nature. In the regulating of its activity, there is a crucial element of choice, therefore, a personal responsibility.

The Mind is the Basic Tool of Survival

Like every other species capable of awareness, we depend for our survival and well-being on the guidance of our distinctive form of consciousness, the form uniquely human, our conceptual faculty—the faculty of abstraction, generalization, and integration. This form of consciousness is what I understand by the term "mind." Its essence is our ability to reason, which means to grasp relationships. Our lives and well-being depend on the appropriate use of our minds.

Mind is more than immediate, explicit awareness. It is a complex architecture of structures and processes. It includes more than the verbal, literal, analytical processes popularly, if misleadingly, described sometimes as "left brain" activity.

It includes the totality of mental life, including the subconscious, the intuitive, the symbolic, all of which is sometimes associated with "right brain." Mind is all the means by which we reach out and apprehend the world.

The Process of Thought

To learn to grow food, to construct a bridge, to harness electricity, to grasp the healing possibility of some substance, to allocate resources so as to maximize productivity, to see wealth-producing possibilities where they had not been seen before, to conduct a scientific experiment, to create, all require a process of thought. To respond appropriately to the complaints of a child or a spouse, to recognize that there is a disparity between our behavior and our professed feelings, to discover how to deal with hurt and anger in ways that will heal, rather than destroy, all require a process of thought.

Even to know when to abandon conscious effort and problem solving and turn the task over to the subconscious. To know when to allow conscious thinking to stop or when to attend more closely to feelings or intuition [subconscious, perceptions, or integrations] require a process of thought, a process of rational connection.

To Think Or Not To Think—A Choice

This is the problem and the challenge. Although thinking is a necessity of successful existence, we are not programmed to think automatically. We have a choice.

We are not responsible for controlling the activities of our heart, lungs, liver, or kidneys. They are all part of the body's self-regulating system [although we are beginning to learn that some measure of control of these activities may be possible for us]. Nor are we obliged to supervise the homeostatic processes, which, for instance, maintain our more or less constant temperature. Nature has designed the organs and systems of our bodies to function automatically in the service of our life without our volitional intervention.

But our minds operate differently. Our minds do not pump knowledge as our hearts pump blood, when and as needed. Our minds do not automatically guide us to act on our best, most rational informed understanding, even when such understanding would clearly be beneficial.

We do not begin to think "instinctively" merely because non-thinking in a given situation becomes dangerous to us. Consciousness does not "reflexively" expand in the face of the new and unfamiliar. Sometimes, we contract it instead. Nature has given us an extraordinary responsibility with the option of turning the searchlight of consciousness brighter or dimmer. This is the option of seeking awareness or not bothering to seek it or actively avoiding it. The option of thinking or not thinking. This is the root of our freedom and our responsibility.

We Can Make Rational or Irrational Choices

We are the one species who can formulate a vision of what values are worth pursuing and then pursue the opposite. We can decide that a given course of action is rational, moral, and wise and then suspend consciousness and proceed to do something else.

We are able to monitor our behavior and ask if it is consistent with our knowledge, convictions, and ideals. And we are also able to evade asking that question—the option of thinking or not thinking.

If I have reason to know that alcohol is dangerous to me and I, nonetheless, take a drink, I must first turn down the light of consciousness. If I know that cocaine has cost me my last three jobs and I, nonetheless, choose to take a snort, I must blank out my knowledge, must refuse to see what I see and know what I know. If I recognize that I am in a relationship that is destructive to my dignity, detrimental to my self-esteem, and dangerous to my physical well-being; and I nonetheless choose to remain in it, I must drown out awareness, fog my mind, and make myself functionally stupid. Self-destruction is an act best performed in the dark.

Our Choices Affect Our Self-Esteem

The choices we make concerning the operations of our consciousness have enormous ramifications for our lives in general and our self-esteem in particular. Consider the impact on our lives and on our sense of self-entailment by the following options:

- Focusing versus non-focusing

- Thinking versus non-thinking

- Awareness versus unawareness

- Clarity versus obscurity or vagueness

- Respect for reality versus avoidance of reality

- Respect for facts versus indifference to facts

- Respect for truth versus rejection of truth

- Perseverance in the effort to understand versus abandonment of the effort

- Loyalty in action to our confessed convictions versus disloyalty to the issue of integrity

- Honesty with self versus dishonesty

- Self-confrontation versus self-avoidance

- Self-critique versus non-self-critique

- Receptivity to new knowledge versus closed mindedness

- Willing to see and correct errors versus perseverance in the error

- Concern with congruence versus disregard of contradictions

- Reason versus rationalism

- Respect for logic, consistency, coherence, and evidence versus disregard or defiance

- Loyalty to the responsibility of conscientiousness versus betrayal of that responsibility

If one wishes to understand the foundations of genuine self-esteem, this list is a good place to begin.

Consciousness, Responsibility, Moral Choices

The point is not that our self-esteem "should" be affected by the choices we make. But rather, by our nature, it must be affected. If we develop habit patterns that cripple or incapacitate us for effective functioning and that causes us to distrust ourselves, it would be irrational to suggest that we "should" go on feeling just as efficacious and worthy as we would feel if our choices had been better. This would imply that our actions have, or should have, nothing to do with how we feel about ourselves. It is one thing to caution against identifying oneself with a particular behavior. It is another to assert that there should be no connection between self-assessment and behavior.

A disservice is done to people if they are offered "feel good" notions of self-esteem that divorce it from questions of consciousness, responsibility, or moral choice. It is the fact that we have choices such as I have described. We are confronted by options encountered nowhere else in nature, and we are the one species able to betray and act against our means of survival. This creates our need for self-esteem, which is the need to know we are functioning as our life and well-being require.

Simply stated, our choices will enhance or harm our self-esteem. We have the option of "choice." Unfortunately, that "choice" does not include the capacity to divorce "choice" from consequence. We are the sum of our choices. Those choices either add up to healthy self-esteem or they do not. The choices we make are within our control—the consequences are not.

If our behavior [choices] devalues us, we cannot merely "choose" not to be devalued. Instead, we must learn to "choose" behaviors which build and sustain healthy self-esteem.

The Next Level:
Self-Esteem and Achievement

Self-esteem is not a free gift that we need only claim. To acquire healthy self-esteem is a true achievement that occurs only over time. To qualify as authentic self-esteem, the experience I am describing must be reality based. It is more than simply a matter of "feeling good about oneself." A state that, at least temporarily, can be induced in any number of ways from having a pleasant sexual encounter to buying a new outfit to receiving a compliment to ingesting certain drugs. Genuine self-efficacy and self-respect asks far more of us than this.

In a current magazine an article appeared that stated, "a standardized math test was given to thirteen year olds in six countries last year. Koreans did the best. Americans did the worst, coming in behind Spain, Ireland, and Canada. Now the bad news—besides being shown triangles and equations, the kids were shown the statement 'I am good at mathematics.' Americans were number one with an impressive sixty-eight percent in agreement. American students may not know their math, but they had evidently absorbed the lessons of the newly fashioned self-esteem curriculum wherein kids are taught to feel good about themselves."

Given the limits of this naïve understanding of self-esteem, the criticisms of "self-esteem curriculum," the author of this article goes on to make are justified. Therefore, when I write of self-efficacy or self-respect, I do so in the context of reality, not of feelings generated out of wishes or affirmations.

One of the characteristics of people with healthy self-esteem is that they begin to assess their abilities and accomplishments realistically, neither denying nor exaggerating them.

How can a student do poorly in school and yet have good self-esteem? Of course, there are any number of reasons why a particular boy or girl might not do well scholastically, including lack of adequate challenge and stimulation. Grades are hardly a reliable indicator of a given individual's self-efficacy and self-respect, though they are certainly an indication of knowledge on a particular subject. But rationally, self-esteeming students do not delude themselves that they are doing well when they are doing poorly.

Schools should, indeed, be concerned to introduce self-esteem principles and practices in their curriculum and there are some excellent programs now in place. But we do not serve the healthy development of young people when we convey that self-esteem may be achieved by reciting "I am special," everyday or by stroking ones own face while saying "I love me," or by identifying self-worth with membership in a particular group [ethnic pride] rather with personal character.

On this last point, let us remember that self-esteem pertains to that which is open to our volitional choice. It cannot properly be a function of the family we were born into or our race or the color of our skin or the achievement of our ancestors. These are values people sometimes cling to in order to avoid responsibility for achieving authentic self-esteem. They are sources of what below I call "pseudo self-esteem."

Can one ever take legitimate pleasure in any of these values? Of course. Can they ever provide temporary support for fragile, growing egos? Probably. But they are not substitutes for consciousness, responsibility, or integrity. They are not sources for self-efficacy and self-respect. They can, however, become sources of self-delusion.

But Is It Authentic?

Sometimes we see people who enjoy worldly success, who are widely esteemed, and who have a public veneer of assurance, yet, are deeply dissatisfied, anxious, or depressed. They may project the appearance of self-esteem, but do not possess the reality. How might we understand them?

Let us begin with the observation that to the extent that we fail to develop authentic self-esteem, the consequences are varying degrees of anxiety, insecurity, self-doubt. This is the sense of being, in effect, inappropriate to existence [although no one thinks of themselves in these terms, instead, one might feel something is "wrong" with me]. This state is extremely painful and because it is painful, we are motivated to evade it, to deny our fears, rationalize our behaviors, and fake a self-esteem we may not possess. We may develop what is often termed pseudo self-esteem.

Pseudo self-esteem is the illusion of self-efficacy and self-respect without the reality. It is a non-rational, self-protected device to diminish anxiety and to provide a spurious sense of security to assuage our need for authentic self-esteem by allowing the real causes of its lack to be evaded.

It is based on values that may be appropriate or inappropriate, but that in either case, are not intrinsically related to that which genuine self-efficacy and self-respect require. For example, instead of seeking self-esteem through consciousness, responsibility, and integrity, a person may seek it through popularity, prestige, material acquisition, or sexual exploits. Instead of valuing personal authenticity, we may value belonging to the right clubs or the right church or the right political party. Instead of practicing appropriate self-assertion, we may practice blind loyalty to a particular group. Instead of seeking self-respect through honesty, we may seek it through philanthropy [I must be a good person, I do good works].

Instead of striving for the power of competence, we may pursue the "power" of manipulating or controlling other people. The possibilities for self-deception are almost endless—all the blind alleys down which we can lose ourselves, not realizing that what we desire cannot be purchased with counterfeit currency.

Self-esteem is an intimate experience that resides in the core of my being. It is what I think and feel about myself, not what someone else thinks and feels about me. This simple fact can hardly be overstressed.

I can be loved by my family, my mate, and my friend, and yet not love myself. I can be admired by my associates, yet regard myself as worthless. I can project an image of assurance and poise that fools virtually everyone, and yet secretly tremble with the sense of my inadequacy. I can fulfill the expectations of others and yet fail my own. I can win every honor, yet feel I have accomplished nothing. I can be adored by millions, and yet wake up each morning with a sickening sense of fraudulence and emptiness.

To attain "success" without attaining positive self-esteem is to be condemned to feeling like an impostor, anxiously awaiting exposure.

Acclaim Is Not Self-Esteem

The acclaim of others does not create our self-esteem. Neither do knowledge, skills, material possessions, parenthood, philanthropic endeavors, sexual conquests, or face lifts. These things can sometimes make us feel better about ourselves temporarily, or more comfortable in particular situations, but comfort is not self-esteem.

Unfortunately, teachers of self-esteem are no less impervious to the worship of false gods than anyone else. I recall listening to a lecture by a man who conducts self-esteem seminars. He announced that one of the very best ways to raise our self-esteem was to surround ourselves with people who think highly of us. I thought of the nightmare of low self-esteem persons surrounded by praise and adulation, like rock stars who have no idea how they got where they are and cannot survive a day without drugs.

I thought of the futility of telling a person of low self-esteem, who feels lucky if he or she is accepted by anyone, that the way to raise self-esteem is to seek the company only of admirers. Clearly, it is wiser to seek companions who are the friends of ones self-esteem, rather than its enemies.

Nurturing relationships are preferable to toxic relationships, but to look to others as a primary source of self-esteem is dangerous. First, because it doesn't work, and second, because we run the risk of becoming approval addicts, which is deadly to mental and emotional well-being.

I do not wish to suggest a psychologically healthy person is unaffected by the feedback he or she receives from others. In fact, we should be impacted by it to some degree. We should factor it in. We are social beings, and certainly others contribute to our self-conceptions, but there are gigantic differences among people in the relative importance to their self-esteem of the feedback they receive. Persons for whom it is almost the only factor of importance and for persons for whom the importance is a good deal less. This is merely another way of saying there are gigantic differences among people in the degree of their autonomy.

Having worked for over twenty-five years with persons who are unhappily preoccupied with the opinions of others, I am persuaded that the most effective means of liberation is by raising the level of consciousness one brings to one's own experience. The more one turns up the volume on one's inner signals, the more external signals tend to recede into proper balance.

This entails, I believe, learning to listen to the body, learning to listen to the emotions, learning to think for oneself.

Authentic Pride

Self-esteem pertains to the experience of our fundamental competence and value. Pride pertains to the more explicitly conscious pleasure we take in ourselves because of our actions and achievements. Self-esteem contemplates what needs to be done and says, "I can." Pride contemplates what has been accomplished and says, "I did."

Authentic pride has nothing in common with bragging, boasting, or arrogance. It comes from an opposite root. Not emptiness, but satisfaction is its wellspring. It is not out to "prove," but to enjoy. Pride is the emotional reward of achievement. It is not a vice to overcome, but a value to be attained.

Does achievement always result in pride? Not necessarily as the following story illustrates:

The head of a medium-sized company consulted me because he said that although he had made a great success of his business, he was depressed and unhappy. He could not understand why. We discovered that what he had always wanted to be was a research scientist, but that he had abandoned that desire in deference to his parents who pushed him toward a career in business.

Not only was he unable to feel more than the most superficial kind of pride in his accomplishments, but he was also wounded in his self-esteem. The reason was not difficult to identify. In the most important issue of his life, he had surrendered his mind and values to the wishes of others, out of the wish to be "loved" and to "belong."

Clearly a still earlier self-esteem problem motivated such a capitulation. His depression reflected a lifetime of performing brilliantly, while ignoring his deepest needs. While he operated within that framework, pride and satisfaction were beyond his reach. Until he was willing to challenge that framework and to face the fear of doing so, no solution was possible for him.

This is an important point to understand because we sometimes hear people say, "I have accomplished so much, why don't I feel more proud of myself?" Although there are several reasons why someone may not enjoy his or her achievements, it can be useful to ask, "Who chose your goals, you or someone you were seeking to please?"

Neither pride nor self-esteem can be supported by the pursuit of second-hand values that do not reflect who we really are, or more importantly, how we truly feel about the world around us.

Volitional Choice—What We Are Willing To Do

As far as our own actions and behavior are concerned, our self-esteem depends to a very great extent, on what we are willing to do. I stress this aspect of volitional choice because there is reason to believe that we may come into this world with certain inherent differences that make it easier or harder to attain healthy self-esteem, differences pertaining to energy, resilience, disposition to enjoy life, and the like. I suspect that in future years, we will learn that our genetic inheritance is definitely part of the story, even to a greater degree than to which we understand it to be today. And certainly, upbringing can play a powerful role. No one can say how many individuals suffer such damage in the early years before the psyche is fully formed. But it is all but impossible for healthy self-esteem to emerge later, short of intense psychotherapy.

Research suggests that one of the best ways to have good self-esteem is to have parents who have good self-esteem and who model it. In addition, we need parents who raise us with love and respect, who allow us to experience consistent and benevolent acceptance, and who give us the supporting structure of reasonable rules and appropriate expectations. We need parents who do not assail us with contradictions, who do not resort to ridicule, humiliation, or physical abuse as a means of controlling us, who project that they believe in our competence and goodness, and then we have a decent chance of internalizing their attitudes and, thereby, acquiring the foundation for healthy self-esteem.

But no research study has ever found this result to be inevitable. Most studies clearly show that this is not the case. There are people who appear to have been raised superbly by the standards indicated above, and yet who are insecure, self-doubting adults. And there are people who have emerged from appalling backgrounds, raised by adults who did everything wrong, yet they do well in school, form stable and satisfying relationships, have a powerful sense of their own value and dignity, and as adults, satisfy any rational criteria of good self-esteem. It is as if they were put on earth to baffle and confound psychiatrists.

While we may not know all the biological and developmental factors that influence self-esteem, we do know a good deal about the specific [volitional] practices that can raise or lower it. We know that an honest commitment to understanding inspires self-trust and that an avoidance of the effort has the opposite effect. We know that people who live mindfully feel more competent than those who live mindlessly. We know that integrity engenders self-respect and that hypocrisy does not. We know all this implicitly, although it is astonishing how rarely such matters are discussed.

Supporting Self-Esteem

We cannot work on self-esteem directly, neither our own or anyone else's because self-esteem is a consequence, a product of internally generated practices, such as that of living consciously, responsibly, purposefully, and with integrity. If we understand what those practices are, we can commit to initiating them within ourselves and to dealing with others in such a way as to facilitate or encourage them to do likewise.

To encourage self-esteem in the family, the school, or the workplace, for instance, is to create an environment that supports and reinforces the practices that strengthen self-esteem.

How Does Self-Esteem Manifest

There are fairly simple and direct ways in which healthy self-esteem manifests itself in our being:

- A face, manner, way of talking and moving that projects the pleasure one takes in being alive.

- Ease in talking of accomplishments or shortcomings with directness and honesty since one is in friendly relationship with the facts.

- Comfort in giving and receiving compliments, expressions of affections, appreciation, and the like.

- Openness to criticism and comfortable about acknowledging mistakes because one's self-esteem is not tied to the image of "perfection."

- One's words and movement tend to have a quality of ease and spontaneity since one is not at war with one's self.

- Harmony between what one says and does and how one looks, sounds, and moves.

- Openness to and curiosity about new ideas, new experiences, and new possibilities.

- Feelings of anxiety or insecurity, if they present themselves, will be less likely to intimidate or overwhelm one since accepting them, managing them, and rising above them rarely feels impossibly difficult.

- An ability to enjoy the numerous aspects of life in one's self and others.

- Flexible in responding to situations and challenges, moved by a spirit of inventiveness and even playfulness since one trusts ones mind and does not see life as doomed or defeat.

- Comfort with assertive [not belligerent] behavior in oneself and others.

- Ability to preserve a quality of harmony and dignity under conditions of stress.

Then on the purely physical level, one can often observe characteristics such as these:

- Eyes are alert, bright, and lively.

- A face is relaxed and [barring illness] tends to exhibit natural color and good skin vibrancy.

- A chin is held naturally in alignment with ones body.

- Jaw is relaxed.

- Shoulders are relaxed, yet erect.

- Hands are relaxed, graceful, and quiet.

- Arms hang in a relaxed, natural way.

- Posture is relaxed, erect, well balanced.

- A walk that is purposeful without being aggressive or overbearing.

- Voice is modulated with intensity appropriate to the situation and with clear pronunciation.

Notice that the theme of relaxation occurs again and again. Relaxation implies that we are not hiding from ourselves and are not at war with who we are. Chronic tension conveys a message of some form of internal split, some form of self-avoidance, or self-repudiation, one aspect of the self being disowned or held on a very tight leash.

How Much Is Enough Self-Esteem?

Is it possible to have too much self-esteem? No it is not. No more than it is possible to have too much physical health. Sometimes self-esteem is confused with boasting or bragging or arrogance, but such traits reflect not too much self-esteem, but too little. They reflect a lack of self-esteem.

People of high self-esteem are not driven to make themselves superior to others; they do not seek to prove their value by measuring themselves against a comparative standard. Their joy is in being who they are, not in being better than someone else.

Engendering Resentment in the Less Secure

True enough, people with troubled self-esteem are often uncomfortable in the presence of high self-esteem people. They may even feel resentful and declare, "They have too much self-esteem," or use some other way to characterize what makes them uncomfortable.

Insecure men, for instance, often feel more insecure in the presence of self-confident women. Low self-esteem individuals often feel irritable in the presence of people who are enthusiastic about life. If one marriage partner has deteriorating self-esteem and sees the other partner's self-esteem growing, the response is sometimes anxiety in an attempt to abort the growth process. The sad truth is, whoever is successful in this world runs the risk of being a target. People of low achievement often envy, and resent people of high achievement. Those who are unhappy often envy and resent those who are happy. Those of low self-esteem sometimes like to talk about the danger of having "too much self-esteem."

The Next Level:
The Sources of Self-Esteem

I remember as a child being enormously bewildered by the behavior of adults. I was often baffled by what I perceived as the strangeness and superficiality of their values. I saw an incongruity between statements and feelings. I experienced an anxiety that seemed to saturate much of the atmosphere around me. It seemed to me that often the adults in my life did not know what they were doing, that they were lost and helpless, while at the same time, they pretended to be in complete control.

This experience was painful and at times, frightening. As a child, like most children, I wanted desperately to understand why human beings behaved as they did. Somewhere in my mind, at quite a young age, there must have been the conviction, that knowledge is power, safety, security, and serenity. Doubtless, this conviction played a significant role in my own personal and professional development.

All of us know times of bewilderment, despair, and a painful sense of impotence or inadequacy. The question is do we allow such moments to define us. It's not that people of healthy self-esteem do not suffer or sometimes know anxiety, but they are not stopped by such experiences. They do not identify themselves with their fear or pain, just as if they got sick, they would not identify themselves with their sickness. They do not see suffering as the essence of life.

Living Consciously, Responsibly, With Integrity

The need for self-esteem arises from the fact that the function of our consciousness is volitional, which confers upon us a unique task—that of making ourselves competent to cope with the challenges of life. We achieve this by living consciously, responsibly, and with integrity. We should judge ourselves by that which is in our volitional control, as I have already stressed. To judge ourselves by that which depends on the will and choices of others, is clearly dangerous to our self-esteem. The tragedy of millions of people is that this is just what they do.

Self-esteem pertains to the issue of our fundamental appropriateness to life and, therefore, to the mental operations that lie behind our behavior. If this is understood, we can readily appreciate the error of measuring our worth by such standards as our popularity, influence, affluence, material possessions, or good looks.

Since we are social beings, some measure of esteem from others is necessary. But tying our self-assessment to the good opinion of others is to place ourselves at their mercy in the most humiliating way. The desire to "please" and, therefore, to avoid disapproval, can lead us to do things that betray our self-esteem. And what are we to do when the people whose esteem we desire have different expectations so that to gain the approval of one's significant other would be to risk the disapproval of another.

There again, we may take pleasure in an attractive appearance, but to tie our self-esteem to our appearance is to be in growing terror with every passing year as the marks of age inevitably advance upon us. And if our good looks are superior to our behavior, they will hardly heal the psychic wounds inflicted by dishonesty, irresponsibility, or irrationality.

A Commitment to Awareness; the Will to Understand

Whenever we see men and women of high self-esteem, we see a high commitment to awareness as a way of life. They live mindfully. They are concerned to know what they are doing when they act, to understand themselves and the world around them, including the feedback they receive which informs them whether they are on course or off course with regard to their goals and purposes. This is what I think should be called the "will to understand."

The potential range of our awareness depends on the extent of our intelligence and the breadth of our abstract capacity, which means our ability to grasp relationships [to see the connection between things]. But the principle of commitment to awareness for the "will to understand" remains the same on all levels of intelligence. It entails the behavior of seeking to integrate, that which enters our mental field, as well as the effort to keep expanding that field.

The beginning of self-assertion is the assertion of consciousness itself—the act of seeing and of seeking to grasp that which we see, of hearing and of seeking to grasp that which we hear, or responding to life actively rather than passively. This is the foundation of healthy self-esteem.

The Bewildering World of Adults

Many children undergo experiences that place enormous obstacles in the way of the healthy development of this attitude. The child may find the world of parents and other adults incomprehensible, even threatening. The self is not nurtured, but attacked. After a number of unsuccessful attempts to understand adult policies, statements, and behaviors, some children give up and take the blame for their feelings of helplessness. Often they sense, miserably, desperately, and inarticulately, that there is something terribly wrong with their elders, or with themselves, or with something, which they cannot quite name.

What they often come to feel is "I'll never understand people. I'll never be able to do what they expect of me. I don't know what's right or wrong, and I'm never going to know."

Developing a Powerful Source of Strength

The child who continues to struggle to make sense out of the world and the people in it, however, is developing a powerful sense of strength, no matter what the anguish or bewilderment experienced.

Caught in a particularly cruel, frustrating, and irrational environment, he or she will doubtless feel alienated from many of the people in the immediate surrounding world, and legitimately so.

But the child will not feel alienated from reality; will not feel, at the deepest level, incompetent to live. The growing individual who retains commitment to awareness learns subjects, acquires skills, accomplishes tasks, and reaches goals. And of course, these successes validate and reinforce the choice to think. The sense of being appropriate to life feels natural. A commitment to awareness, a commitment to rationality, to consciousness, and a respect for reality as a way of life is both a source and expression of positive self-esteem.

Often we associate positive self-esteem only with the result—with knowledge, success, the admiration and appreciation of others, and miss the cause: all the choices that cumulatively add up to what we call a commitment to awareness, the will to understand. We thus can deceive ourselves about the actual sources of self-esteem.

The Will to Be Efficacious

When we see self-esteem, we see what I call "the will to be efficacious." The concept of the will to be efficacious is an extension of the will to understand. It places its emphasis on perseverance in the face of difficulties, continuing to seek understanding, and understanding does not come easily, pursuing the mastery of a skill or the solution of a problem in the face of defeat, maintaining a commitment to goals while encountering many obstacles along the way.

The will to be efficacious is the refusal to identify our ego or self with momentary feelings of helplessness and defeat. The will to be efficacious is the refusal of a human consciousness to accept helplessness as its permanent and unalterable condition.

Strategic Detachment—Knowing You Are More Than Your Problems

It is impressive to see a person who has been battered by life in many ways, who is torn by a variety of unsolved problems, who may be alienated from many aspects of the self, and yet who is still fighting, still struggling, still striving to find the path to a more fulfilling existence moved by the wisdom of knowing "I am more than my problems."

Children who survive extremely adverse childhoods have learned a particular survival strategy that relates to the issue we are discussing. I call it, "strategic detachment." This is not the withdrawal from reality that leads to psychological disturbance, rather an intuitively calibrated disengagement from noxious or poison aspects of their family life or other aspects of their world. They somehow know this is not all there is. They hold the belief that a better alternative exists somewhere and that someday they will find their way to it. They persevere in that idea. They somehow know mother is not all women, father is not all men, and this family does not exhaust the possibilities of human relationships. There is life beyond this neighborhood.

This does not spare them suffering in the present, but it allows them not to be destroyed by it. Their strategic detachment does not guarantee that they will never have feelings of powerlessness, but it helps them not to be stuck there. Whether as children or adults, having the will to be efficacious does not mean that we deny or disown feelings of inefficacy when they arise. It means that we do not accept them as permanent. We feel temporarily helpless without defining our essence as helplessness. We can feel temporarily defeated without defining our essence as failure. We can allow ourselves to feel temporarily hopeless, overwhelmed, while preserving the knowledge that after a rest, we will pick up the pieces as best we can and start moving forward again.

Our vision of our life extends beyond the feelings of the moment. Our concept of self can rise above today's adversity. This is one of the forms of heroism possible to a volitional consciousness.

Self-Esteem and IQ

No study, that I am aware of, has ever suggested that good self-esteem correlates with IQ. And this is not surprising. Self-esteem is a function, not of our natural endowment, but of our manner of using our consciousness—the choices we make concerning awareness, the honesty of our relationship to reality, the level of our personal integrity.

Self-esteem is neither competitive nor comparative. Its context is always the individual's relationship to self and to the choices of self. A person of high intelligence and high self-esteem does not feel more appropriate to life or more worthy of happiness than a person of high self-esteem and more modest intelligence.

An analogy may prove helpful. Two people may be equally healthy and physically fit, but one is stronger than the other. The one who is stronger does not experience a higher level of physical well-being. One can merely do some things the other cannot. Looking at them from outside, we may say that one enjoys certain advantages over the other, but this does not mean that there is a difference in the internal feeling of wellness and aliveness.

Thinking Independently

Intellectual independence is implicit in the commitment of awareness or the will to understand. A person cannot think through the mind of another. We can learn from one another, but knowledge entails understanding, not mere repetition or imitation. We can either exercise our own mind or pass on to others the responsibility for knowledge and evaluation and accept their verdicts more or less uncritically. The choice we make is crucial for the way we experience ourselves and for the kind of life we create.

Goals and Intentions Are Crucial

That we are sometimes influenced by others in ways we do not recognize does not alter the fact that there is a distinction between the psychology of those who try to understand things for themselves, think for themselves, judge for themselves, and those to whom such a possibility rarely occurs. What is crucial here is the matter of intention, the matter of an individual's goal.

I recall a person who once said to me, "I can't understand why I'm always relying on the opinions of other people." I asked her, "As you were growing up, did you ever want to be independent, and did you ever make independence your goal?" She pondered for a moment and then replied, "No." I said, "No need to be surprised then that you didn't arrive there."

To speak of "thinking independently" is useful because independency has value in terms of emphasis. Often what people call "thinking" is merely recycling the opinions of others. So we can say that thinking independently about our work, our relationships, the values that will guide our lives, and the goals we will set for ourselves is a generator of self-esteem. And healthy self-esteem results in a natural inclination to think independently.

Self-Esteem is Acquired, Not Given

Seeing only the tail end of the process I am describing, a person might say, "It's easy for him to think independently, look at how much self-esteem he has." But self-esteem is not given, it is acquired. One of the many ways self-esteem is acquired is by thinking independently when it may not be easy to do so or when it may be frightening. When the person doing the thinking struggles with feelings of uncertainty and insecurity and chooses to persevere nonetheless, the person's self-esteem will increase.

It is not always easy to stand by our judgment and if it has become easy, that itself is a psychological victory, because in the past, there were certainly times when it was not easy, when the pressures against independent thought were considerable and when we had to confront and endure anxiety. When a child finds that his or her perceptions, feelings, or judgment conflict with those of parents or other family members and the child must choose whether to heed the voice of self or to disown it in favor of the voice of others.

When a woman believes that her husband is wrong on some fundamental issue, she must choose whether to express her thoughts or to suppress them and thus protect the "closeness" of the relationship. When an artist or scientist suddenly sees a path that would carry him or her far from the consensual beliefs and values of colleagues, far from the mainstream of contemporary orientation and opinion, the artist must choose whether to follow that lonely path, wherever it leads, or to draw back. The issue and the challenge in all such situations remain the same—should one honor one's inner signals or disown them. Independence versus conformity, self-expression versus self-repudiation, self-assertion versus self-surrender.

The Heroism of Consciousness

While it may sometimes be necessary, we do not normally enjoy long periods of being alienated from the thinking and beliefs of those around us, especially those we respect and love. One of the most important forms of heroism is the heroism of consciousness, the heroism of thought, and the willingness to tolerate loneliness.

Like every other psychological trait, independence is a matter of degree. No one is perfectly independent and no one is hopelessly dependent all of the time. The higher the level of our independence and the more willing we are to think for ourselves, and then the higher our self-esteem will be.

Learning to Discriminate

No one can feel properly efficacious [that is, competent to cope with the basic challenges of life] who has not learned to differentiate between facts on one hand and wishes and fears on the other. The task is sometimes difficult because thoughts themselves are invariably touched or saturated with feeling.

Still, on many occasions, we can recognize that the desire to perform some action is not proof that we should perform it. For example, running out of the room in the midst of an argument when you become upset is not desirable. And the fact that we may be afraid to perform some action is not proof that we should avoid performing it. Going to a physician for a checkup when there are signs of illness is another example. If we make a purchase we know we cannot afford and avoid thinking about impending bills we will not be able to pay, we have surrendered our consciousness to our wishes.

If we ignore signs of danger in a marriage and then profess to be bewildered and dismayed when the bridge finally explodes, we have paid the penalty for sacrificing consciousness to fear.

Our Underlying Intentions

As far as self-esteem is concerned, the issue is not whether we are flawless in executing the task of distinguishing among facts, wishes, and fears, and choosing consciousness over some form of avoidance. Rather, the issue is one of underlying intention.

When we describe a person as "basically honest," in the sense meant here, we do not mean that he or she is impervious to the influence of wishes and fears, but rather that there is a pronounced and evident desire and intention to see things as they are. We cannot always know for certain whether or not we are being rational or honest, but we can certainly be concerned about it. We can certainly care. We are not always free to succeed in our thinking, but we are always free to try.

The accumulated sum of our choices in this matter yields an inner sense of basic honesty or dishonesty, the fundamental responsibility or irresponsibility toward existence. From childhood on, some individuals are far more interested in and respectful of such questions of truth than others.

Some operate as if facts need not be facts if we do not choose to acknowledge them, as if truth is irrelevant, and lies are lies only if someone finds them out. The bottom line is that to honor reality is to honor self-esteem.

Integrity

Where we see self-esteem, we see behavior that is consistent to the individual's professed values, convictions, and beliefs. We see integrity. When we behave in ways that conflict with our judgments of what is appropriate, we lose face in our own eyes. We respect ourselves less. If the policy becomes habitual, we trust ourselves less or cease to trust ourselves at all.

In their eagerness to disassociate themselves from philosophy in general and ethics in particular, psychologists are often uncomfortable with anything that sounds like a reference to morality in the context of psychotherapy or psychological well-being. In consequence, they can miss the obvious fact. Integrity is, in effect, one of the guardians of mental health. It is cruel and misleading to encourage people to believe that practicing "unconventional positive regard" toward themselves will bring them to self-love, irrespective of the question of their personal integrity.

Values, Principles, and Standards

Sometimes an individual seeks to escape from the burden of integrity by disavowing or professing to disavow all values and standards. The truth is human beings cannot successfully regress to a lower level of evolution. We cannot draw back to a time before thinking and principles and long-range planning were possible. We are conceptual beings. That is our nature and we cannot function successfully as anything less.

We need values to guide our actions. We need principles to guide our lives. Our standards may be appropriate or inappropriate to the requirements of our lives and well-being, but to live without standards of any kind is impossible.

A Code of Values

We may accept a code of values that does violence to our needs as living organisms. For example, certain religious teachings implicitly or explicitly condemn sex, condemn pleasure, condemn the body, condemn ambition, condemn material success, and condemn [for all practical purposes] the enjoyment of life on earth. This acceptance of life-denying standards is an enormous problem and one that I think we cannot escape if we are honest with ourselves.

Here, I will simply observe, that once we see that living up to our standards appears to be leading us toward self-destruction, the time has obviously come to question our standards, rather than simply resigning ourselves to living without integrity. We may need to summon up the courage to challenge some of our deepest assumptions concerning what we have been taught to regard as good.

Self-Acceptance

Where we see self-esteem, we see self-acceptance. High self-esteem individuals tend to avoid falling into adversarial relationships with themselves. If we are to grow and change, we must begin by learning self-acceptance. In my experience, self-acceptance is not an easy concept for most people to understand. The tendency is to equate self-acceptance with the approval of every aspect of our personality [or physical appearance] and with the denial that any change or improvement might be desirable.

To be self-accepting does not mean to be without a wish to change, improve, or evolve. It means not to be at war with ourselves, not to deny the reality of what is true of us right now, at this moment of our existence.

To accept ourselves is to accept the fact that what we think, feel, and do are all expressions of the self at the time they occur. If we cannot accept the fact of what we are at any given moment of our existence, if we cannot permit ourselves fully to be aware of the nature of our

choices and actions, if we cannot admit the truth into our consciousness, we cannot change.

The Power of Self-Responsibility

Working with people from all walks of life, I am intrigued when I
catch the moment at which growth suddenly seems to spurt forward. I
often see that the most radical transformation occurs after the person
realizes that "No one is coming to the rescue." Many people have said
to me, "When I finally allowed myself to face fully my responsibility
for my life, then I began to grow, I began to change, and my self-
esteem began to rise."

In reality, we are responsible for our choices and actions. Not
responsible as the recipient of moral blame or guilt, but responsible as
the chief causal agent in our lives and behavior. I do not mean to imply
that a person never suffers through accident or through the fault of
others, nor that a person is responsible for everything in life that may
happen to him or her. We are not omnipotent. But self-responsibility
is clearly indispensable to good self-esteem.

Avoiding self-responsibility victimizes us with regard to our own
lives. It leaves us helpless. It is just this view from which many people
need to emancipate themselves if they are ever to evolve to a non-tragic
sense of life. Self-empowerment comes in believing and declaring the
following:

- I am responsible for the attainment of my desires and goals.

- I am responsible for my choices and actions.

- I am responsible for how I deal with people.

- I am responsible for the level of consciousness and conscientiousness
  I bring to my work.

- I am responsible for the decisions by which I live.

• I am responsible for my personal happiness.

Much more remains to be said about the conditions of successful self-esteem, more than can be covered in this writing alone. What I have offered here are some general observations concerning the fundamentals of self-esteem.

The Roots of Self-Esteem Are Internal

Self-esteem is rooted internally in mental operations rather than external successes or failures. This is an essential point to understand. The failure to understand this principle causes an incalculable amount of unnecessary anguish and self-doubt. If we judge ourselves by criteria that entail factors outside our volitional control, the result, unavoidably, is a precarious self-esteem that is in chronic jeopardy.

But our self-esteem need not be affected or impaired if, in spite of our best efforts, we fail in a particular undertaking, even though we will not experience the same emotion of pride that we would have felt if we had succeeded.

Further, we need to remember that the self is not a static, finished entity, but is continually evolving, creating, and unfolding in our choices, decisions, thoughts, judgments, responses, and actions. To view ourselves as basically and unalterably good or bad, independent of our present and future manner of functioning, is to negate the facts of freedom, self-determination, and self-responsibility. We always contain within ourselves the possibility of change. We need never be the prisoner of yesterday's choices.

The simple reality is that people change when they choose to change. And until they choose to change, they do not change. All else, that is, all else that appears to be change, is simply accommodation.

The Next Level:
Self-Esteem in the Workplace

Self-esteem may be the most important emotional resource we have to help us meet the challenges of the future. That challenge is especially evident in the workplace where it is becoming clear that self-esteem is not an emotional luxury, but a survival requirement.

Recent research is helping to clarify the important role that self-esteem plays in our ability to take risks, learn new skills, be creative, take feedback, deal with others fairly and benevolently, be productive, and assertive. We need to cultivate these important traits in order to function optimally in our families, organizations, and communities. We have reached a moment in history when self-esteem, which has always been a supremely important psychological survival need, has now become a supremely important economic survival need as well.

We have witnessed the shift from a manufacturing society to an information society—and from a domestic economy to a global economy. We live in a time of extraordinarily rapid change, of phenomenal scientific and psychological breakthroughs. Muscle work is becoming a smaller and smaller part of our economic activity. Mind work is on the rise. This is the day of the knowledge worker. New leadership techniques must be developed that are appropriate for leading a better educated, more independent and creative workforce. Even psychotherapists and counselors need greater awareness of these issues as they see more clients with job-related stress.

Developments in the workplace in this time of accelerated change, choices, and challenges demand a greater capacity for innovation, self-management, personal responsibility, and self-direction—all qualities of high self-esteem.

Trusting Yourself

The most fundamental meaning of self-esteem is trust in your own mind, your own mental processes. Therefore, trust in your ability to learn to judge and to decide. So the primary way we can think of self-esteem as a survival need is in the context of realizing that for humans, the mind or conscientiousness is the basic means of survival on which we rely to keep us in contact with reality and guide our behavior appropriately.

An individual who, at a core level, distrusts his or her own mind is at a severe disadvantage in coping with the choices and options that life presents.

Think of positive self-esteem as the immune system of consciousness, providing resistance, strength, and a capacity for regeneration in handling the challenges of life.

The Ability to Make Decisions

Studies conducted among top executives suggest that one of the leading causes of failure is the inability to make decisions. That inability is due to troubled self-esteem. That is, distrusting one's own mind and judgment.

In many situations, a great amount of information must be obtained and analyzed in order for leaders to make good decisions. And certainly the input of others is a contributing factor. Much has been written about the value of making "balanced" decisions, but that must mean more than merely gathering votes. Consensus thinking may actually lead away from innovative choice.

Guidelines for Making Decisions

In my view, decision-making is a matter of looking at the widest possible context when you make your decisions. It is the ability to ask yourself the following:

1. What are all the factors I know of that can conceivably bear upon my decision?

2. What are all of the foreseeable consequences of my decisions?

3. Who is likely to be affected and how?

In other words, a highly conscious person is looking for the greatest amount of relevant input he or she can find to guide the decision-making process. It is not a matter of my decision versus someone else's. It is an issue of respect for fact, respect for truth. One of the hallmarks of healthy self-esteem is a strong reality orientation and then trusting your own mind for making the right decision.

There will be contexts in which healthy self-esteem includes or even demands getting input from others, though that does not necessarily mean taking opinion polls. Someone may be far ahead of the other people involved and able to see things others are not able to see. The Wright Brothers, for example, did not bother to take a poll.

The consensus model of decision-making has its place, but depends, to some extent, on the ability of innovators or visionaries to get their ideas across. Some are not able to articulate the vision clearly enough to get support for what might be the best decision. Some very important ideas are lost to this inability.

For an innovator to put across a new product or technique or management method, a high level of self-esteem is of inestimable value.

Approaching Others in a Benevolent Spirit

People who are happy to be themselves, who trust themselves, and are at peace with themselves are free emotionally and psychologically to approach others in a benevolent spirit. Those with positive self-esteem tend to elicit cooperation, share enthusiasm and consensus more readily than people who are more self-doubting, insecure, and think in terms of a "you versus me or in a win-lose" model of human relationships.

Whenever you are thinking about people in the context of a large organization or in their personal lives, people who trust themselves tend to deal with others with much greater respect and benevolence than do those who do not—with predictable outcomes in terms of their ability to gain cooperation.

The Conviction That We Are Worthy of Success

This also relates to the worthiness component of self-esteem—that conviction that we are worthy and deserving of success, happiness, trust, respect, and love.

All of life consists of pursuing values. To pursue values, I have to value the beneficiary of my values, namely myself. If, at the core, I do not feel worthy of success or happiness, I most likely will not attain it, and if I do, I am unlikely to enjoy it. We often see people at work who feel capable, but not worthy. So they work and work and never feel entitled to rest and enjoy what they have accomplished.

People, who doubt their efficacy and worth, tend to experience fear of other people and, as a consequence, may tend to fall into adversarial relationships with them. Other people are perceived to be a threat.

If, in contrast, we have confidence in our efficacy and worth, we are much less likely to fall into a "you versus me" mentality. We are more likely to form cooperative relationships and be skillful at building consensus.

High Levels of Social Cooperation

People with high self-esteem are not driven to make themselves superior to others. They do not seek to prove their value by measuring themselves against a comparative standard. Their joy is in being who they are, not in being better than someone else.

Feeling As If You Make a Difference

I have worked with a number of unproductive teams over the years. One of the core causes is many of the individuals on such teams feel that they really did not have the capacity to make a difference. They did not think that their contribution was going to count for anything. The more they began to believe their input would matter, the more easily they cooperated with each other. It was clearly an issue of self-esteem.

It is a basic human desire to be visible to others, to be seen and appreciated for who we are. And it is natural to want to work in an environment which supports us, supports our self-esteem, supports the view that our contribution can and will make a difference.

Self-Esteem, Anchored in Our Ability to Learn

Because knowledge is exploding rapidly, all of us, to remain effective, need to have a commitment to life-long learning. For many, this represents a significant shift in attitude. It is not easy to take a more abstract approach in which self-esteem is anchored, not in what we have or know, but in our ability to learn. This is important not only in unstable economic times. Any unpredictable change can force the need to learn something new. It is our comfort level—the ease with which we continue to learn and grow—that drives our individual survival (success) in times of change.

For example, it is more helpful to ask, "How did I go from knowing nothing about engineering [or sales or teaching, etc.] to knowing quite a bit about it? What do I already know about learning unfamiliar things that I can bring to this new challenge?"

High Expectations for Success

Those in a position to coach or train others need to cultivate an appreciation for the ability to learn. In the workplace, leaders need to uphold high expectations for success in themselves and in those they lead, and at the same time, create an environment where it is safe to make responsible mistakes. It is very tricky to create a disciplined, risk taking, non-punitive environment. It can be difficult to hold people to higher levels of expectancy while allowing them to grow and learn. This is not a contradiction, but it does take a lot of careful thinking in order to implement.

You might start with the premise that they are going to have something worthwhile and interesting to say. And if you do not really believe that the person can think and their opinion is worth something, think about how you would act if you did believe it and then practice those behaviors for sixty to ninety days and see if you notice any changes.

Regarding setting high expectations when delegating work, ask the person if they can accomplish this task, if they are willing to be responsible for delivering it, etc. Work to get firm agreement about what has been promised and then review it after the task is done.

Goal Setting Responsibility

Whenever possible, it is best to have a team set its own expectations and goals within the framework of the organization's goals. It strengthens the experience of personal autonomy. And some research says that when groups set their own goals, they tend to set them higher than when others set the goals for them.

Leaders with positive self-esteem have less trouble giving up control of goal setting and other tasks. To implement such leadership techniques as shared goal setting it is probably worthwhile to bring in a self-esteem expert who can really make clear what kind of difference it will make in the workplace and why.

Once people understand how self-esteem operates in the human psyche, they will spot opportunities for application that an outsider would not.

A leader is not a psychotherapist and cannot be expected to be. It has never been my view that leaders should be. And furthermore, employees do not sign on for their leader's psychotherapy even if the leader were so disposed.

Challenge, Stimulate, and Stretch

Studies suggest that we get the best out of people when we ask a little more of them than they think they can do. In other words, we stretch them. We set our sights high, but not so high as to be paralyzing. I think the same high principle can be applied to ourselves. Leaders need to set their self-expectations realistically to be sure, but high enough to challenge, stimulate, and stretch. For every individual whose problem is that he overestimates his abilities, there are a hundred people who underestimate theirs.

No Shortcuts to Self-Esteem

There are no shortcuts to high self-esteem. We cannot cheat reality. If we do not live consciously, authentically, responsibly, and with high integrity, we may be successful, popular, wealthy, and belong to all the right clubs, but we will have only pseudo self-esteem. Self-esteem is always an intimate experience. It is what we think and feel about ourselves, not what someone else thinks and feels. In the final analysis, self-esteem is the reputation we get with ourselves.

0-595-29587-8